White Ally

White Ally

A Guide to Cultivating a Deeply Spiritual AntiRacism Practice

Sonia Roberts

Dedication

This book is dedicated to my grandmothers, Juana Lopez Marquez and Jemmie Swindell. Grandma Jane died when I was four years old, but I've always felt her spirit so strongly in my life. Her creative spirit greatly influenced my desire to breakdown the barrier of what's achievable. Grandmommy Swindell is a pillar of strength. She has overcome so many obstacles and painful circumstances in her life. She reminds me to plant my feet, in the right place, and to stand strong.

And to Black people everywhere, no matter what the world tells you, always remember you are worthy, you are amazing, and you are MAGIC.

Contents

Preface

My granddaddy called me "yellow girl." As a young child, I never understood why. I didn't want to be different than him, or my brother, or my sister, or anyone. I didn't want to be singled out or alienated. In middle school one day, my white friend said, "Well, you're not really Black." And I thought, why not? What is Black? Am I not Black because I don't 'look Black,' 'talk Black,' or 'act Black?' This demeaning, offensive and backhanded compliment stripped away the race from which I had come. Being a light-skinned Black woman forces me into racial ambiguity. I live in between races. However, I identify as Black. It's what I experience in the world, it's how I choose to identify and it's what I feel in my heart. I recognize my light-skin privilege and I embrace my Blackness.

I was born in 1976 in Redwood City, California, to a white race mother of Mexican and Spanish descent and an African American father. Interracial marriage, once outlawed in the United States of America, became legal in the entire United States in 1967, just eight years before my parents were married.

When I was two years old, we moved from an apartment building on the west side of Redwood City to a house in the suburbs. We were the only Black family in the neighborhood. When my parents rented that house, my "white passing" mother purposely went to sign the lease without my Black father. She also left us, her three Black children, in the car, just in case the landlord had any racial bias. Later, when the landlord met my father, he let him know that the neighbor across the street had said to him, "Why are you renting to that nigger? I would hang him by that tree."

Sadly, Jim Crow laws legalized racial segregation and existed for about 100 years from the post-Civil War era until 1968. Segregation not only occurred in the southern states of America; California also has a rich history of discrimination.

"Hail Mary full of grace. The Lord is with thee." I grew up attending Catholic church with my mother and Mexican grandfather. It was a quick one-hour mass of sitting, standing, kneeling, standing again, worshipping rather quietly. I also grew up attending my granddaddy's church, Church of God in Christ (COGIC), a Pentecostal tradition. My father is now the pastor. I come from a long line of pastors and preachers who have a passion for Jesus Christ. I sometimes attended Sunday school followed by three hours of church. Long sermons where my granddaddy preached, walked, ran, and danced around with a microphone, in order to get his biblical message across to the church members. He would be sweating and swaying to the rhythm of the organ. Eventually, someone would "catch" the gift of the holy ghost, dance around uncontrollably and speak in tongues.

One day, my sister and I were playing in our living room. We decided to reenact the experience of catching the holy ghost at church. I may have danced around a little too crazy because I fell and hit my face right on the corner of the coffee table. Blood squirted everywhere, I went to the ER and had to get a few stitches right under my left eye. My father said, "God don't like ugly."

I am grateful I was able to experience two very different religious traditions. My parents always had tremendous faith in God, but as a teenager, I was influenced by mother's shift into a more spiritual path. I witnessed how a spiritual person deeply cares about people and has a strong desire for soul searching reflections. I respect all religions and don't follow any one in particular. I believe in one God, and often say, "Love is my religion."

I deeply care about people. I think the seed of desire to be of service, help improve people's lives and change the world was planted somewhere around middle-school age. That's when I started to read and learn about the pain and suffering in the world and to reflect on my own. I discovered Harlem Renaissance poets and I devoured Langston Hughes, Claude McKay, James Weldon Johnson and Countee Cullen. I was activated by Assata Shakur, Mumia Abu Jamal and Malcolm X. Reading their work helped me learn more about slavery, Black identity, and the effects of institutional racism. It changed my world. During that time, I began to write as a way of healing. I wanted to make a difference in my own life and in the world.

While in college, I continued to work on healing my own trauma and pain. After college, I worked for various non-profits, a rape crisis center, an employment program for low-income girls, a homebuyer assistance center, a center for responsible lending and a sustainability organization. I realized this work is hard and creating change is slow. Witnessing other people's pain and suffering is intense, and often times, holding their pain is worse than feeling your own. I began to understand how much this work is not just about changing the world;

it's about changing myself. The world changes from within. When I found yoga, it gave me life. Right away, I knew I had to teach it. Yoga gave me space to slow down and shift my focus inward. One day at a time, I realized, I can change everything. One person at a time, I can change the world. And so can you.

Slowly, I'm learning to use my voice and not fear the power of my voice. Growing up, I witnessed violence that I believe was created out of the history of enslavement and racism that continues today. I didn't have a voice to fight back. I didn't have an ally. I had to live in fear. I have worked hard at finding my voice that was taken from me. I am committed to fighting for equal rights for all people, fueled by a strong desire to end violence and oppression.

Yoga principles and meditation are transformative practices that can be instrumental in facilitating social change. Yogic principles influenced the approach of civil rights leader Martin Luther King Jr. and anti-apartheid activist Nelson Mandela as they protested segregation and injustices. They both practiced Karma Yoga[1], dedicating their lives to the service of others. They understood that the suffering of one is the suffering of all. Yoga, self-reflection, and mindfulness can be practiced to promote personal transformation and social change throughout the world.

---

[1] In the Bhagavad Gita, four paths of yoga are described. The four paths are: Raja Yoga-the path of meditation; Jnana Yoga-the path of self inquiry; Bhakti Yoga-the path of devotion; Karma Yoga-the path of selfless service.

Introduction

"The true revolutionary is guided by a great feeling of love. It is impossible to think of a genuine revolutionary lacking this quality." ~Che Guevara

The practice of yoga originated in India with the intention of preparing the body as a foundation for unity with the spirit. Yoga is a system that is much more than practicing asanas or yoga postures. The physical postures are just a small part of the practice. It is a way of living designed to heighten your awareness and deepen your experience of oneness of mind, body and soul with the Divine. Through the practice of yoga, you are uncovering your deepest, truest, most authentic and loving self.

I have been deeply inspired and awakened by the practices of yoga, writing and reflecting. This book is a calling to transform your life from a fear-based reality to a reality based in love. Learning how to truly love is how we heal ourselves and the world. Healing is the pathway to integration and wholeness. This book aims to help you live a more meaningful life by deepening your awareness of your true self and the world around you. As you become more mindful and begin to acknowledge systemic racism and injustice, you can use this awareness to become a more effective ally to people of color. In this book, you will learn how to cultivate an anti-racism practice using the framework of yoga's ten guidelines, the Yamas and the Niyamas. Throughout the book, you will examine your biases, conditioning, values and beliefs by exploring the Yamas and Niyamas, practicing guided meditations, mindfulness, and writing reflections. I have deep respect for the ancient tradition of yoga and am applying these simple principles to race awareness.

Yoga and Social Justice: Building a Conscious Community

In the United States, yoga has largely become commodified, often narrowly focused on mastering asanas or physical postures, weight loss and burning calories, and achieving a tight little yoga butt. Yoga practice is more about transforming the human spirit than the human body. The yoga sutras[2] teach us that yoga is so much more than asana. The practice of yoga is intended to transform the human spirit, increasing our awareness of how we move through the world and how we interact with others. Yoga can be a spiritual foundation for social action.

What is social justice?

---

[2] The Yoga Sūtras of Patañjali are a collection of 196 Indian sutras on the theory and practice of yoga.

Social justice is a movement towards a socially just world. It is based on the concepts of fair and just relations between the individual and society. Social justice is necessary as it ensures the fair treatment of all people. It examines the ways in which rights and resources are distributed. Lack of social justice disrupts marginalized communities' access to quality education, healthcare, living wages, a respectable quality of living and other resources.

What is social change?

Social change refers to the notion of social progress. It is the philosophical idea that society moves forward by evolutionary means. Social movements are groups of individuals or organizations that focus on political or social issues. Social movements play an important role in bringing about social change. Yoga and social justice connect to promote inner change and social change.

Why is social justice important?

The concern for the social welfare of both the world and its people is essential to the practice of yoga. We can no longer ignore another Black person being shot by the police, immigrants being rounded up in their own neighborhoods and deported, families seeking asylum and being separated at the border and the president of the United States tweeting bigotry against transgender service members. We can no longer ignore lack of cultural diversity and inclusion, cultural appropriation, and spiritual bypassing in the yoga community and beyond. Talking about these realities in a sacred space like yoga is an opportunity to deepen the consciousness of our communities. As we process collective and cultural pain, we become people who truly can change the world. Having equality and cultural diversity in a society promotes opportunity, growth and social well-being.

Essential Guidelines: What are the Yamas and Niyamas?

The Yamas and Niyamas are guidelines or the blueprint to living your most meaningful life; they offer a core of mindful anti-racism practices. The guidelines are a reminder of the compassionate choices you can make in your thoughts, words and actions. Compassion literally means "to suffer together." It is a feeling that arises with a desire to act, when you are confronted with another's suffering. Compassion is pausing before any thought, word or action, checking your heart and making sure you are speaking, thinking or acting from love.

In yogic philosophy, the Yamas and Niyamas are the first two limbs of the 8-fold path, or Ashtanga yoga.[3] The first five guidelines are called Yamas, a Sanskrit word that means "restraints." The last five are called Niyamas, a Sanskrit word that means "observances."

---

[3] Ashtanga yoga comes from the Yoga Sutras of Patanjali. The other six limbs of the 8-fold path are Asana, or postures; Pranayama, or breath control; Pratyahara, or sense withdrawal; Dharana, or concentration; Dhyana, or meditation; and Samadhi, or a state of unity.

The Philosophy and Practice of Yoga

The path of evolution requires restraint (Yamas) + observation (Niyamas) + action and practice of all eight limbs. Leading to liberation, joy and justice for all.

1 Yamas	2 Niyamas	3 Asana	4 Pranayama
The Five Moral Restraints	*The Five Observances*	*Postures*	*Mindful Breathing*
Ahimsa	Saucha	Physical poses	Expansion of prana
Satya	Santosha	with breath, mind	or life force, vital
Asteya	Tapas	and spirit to create	energy through
Brahmacharya	Svadhyaya	strength,	control of breath
Aparigraha	Ishvara-pranidhana	flexibility, balance, and focus	
5 Pratyahara	6 Dharana	7 Dhyana	8 Samadhi
Turning Inward	*Concentration*	*Meditation*	*Union of Self with Object of Meditation,*
Withdrawal of the	Focusing,	Reflection,	Bliss, Enlightenment,
senses to the mind	Attention	Observation	Spiritual Illumination,
			the Seeker becomes the Seer

*The Ashtanga Yoga System. The eight-limb path of yoga from the Yoga Sutras of Patanjali.

Yamas — Ethical Consideration

Ahimsa — Nonviolence

Satya — Truthfulness

Asteya — Nonstealing

Brahmacharya — Nonexcess

Aparigraha — Nonpossessiveness

1 Ahimsa - Nonviolence/non-harming, practice with your thoughts, words, and actions with others and yourself. Kindness and compassion for yourself and every living being.Work for justice, equality, and fairness. Examine privilege, power, oppression. Anti-racism practice. Self-love.

2 Satya- Truthfulness, realness, follow integrity and compassion to find the truth. Seek the truth for justice and equality. Stand up. Speak up. Code switching.

THE YAMAS

Ethical Considerations

5 Aparigraha- Nonpossessiveness, non-greedy and a generous heart. Realize there's enough for everyone. Detachment equals freedom.Don't take it personal. Let go and trust the process.

4 Brahmacharya- Nonexcess, moderation, sacred balance and right use of energy. Sustain your life-force energy for your spiritual growth. Connecting with God. Mind your Business/ Racism.

3 Asteya- Nonstealing, nonerasing, all good things will come to you. Avoid cultural appropriation and acknowledge power & privilege.

Niyamas — Self Observation

Saucha — Purity

Santosha — Contentment

Tapas — Self-Discipline

Svadhyaya — Self-Study

Ishvara Parnidhana — Surrender

1 Saucha- Purity, clarity, detox. Recognize bad habits that no longer serve you. Explore internalized racism and anti-blackness. Detox from the inside out. Remove toxic people from your life. Discover and embrace who you are.

2 Santosha- Contentment, gratitude, accept and radically love yourself and your life right now. Gratitude = Kind & Loving Heart. Gratitude makes you less self centered/ white centered.

THE NIYAMAS

Self Observation

5 Ishvara-pranidhana- Surrender, Devotion to a higher power. Devote yourself to a cause you are passionate about. Empowerment. Search for meaning in your life.

4 Svadhyaya- Self-study, self-reflection, study of texts. Intense self-inquiry. Deepen your knowledge of self and the world. Examine biases, racial conditioning and update values. Avoid spiritual bypassing and "color blindness."

3 Tapas- Self-discipline, heat, inner fire, passion and courage. Transform lessons into blessings. Challenge yourself to be uncomfortable. Get to the root of your fears.

Yoga means union or to unite. How can we use our yoga practice to heal and unify our country and the world? What I have discovered is how much these guidelines can help you turn your yoga practice into a social and political force for positive change.

Approach Your Writing and Reflections In a Yogic Way

Writing is a great way to review, reflect, and transform your life. In this book, each chapter will explore the meaning of a guideline, a Yama or Niyama. Guided meditations are included at the end of the chapter. You can listen along to the meditations on my website listed below. Each mindful meditation will guide you to reflect and deeply contemplate your being, your relationship to others and oppression. Writing reflections are included at the end of the chapter for you to examine your racial biases, values, thoughts and beliefs. Use this book to cultivate an anti-racism practice and begin aligning your thoughts, words and actions for your personal healing and the healing of the collective whole.

Practice, write and reflect without attachment to the outcome. Get a journal to write down your reflections at the end of each chapter. Be present and patient with your process. For many white people, if you have never paused to examine whiteness and racism, this book may push you out of your comfort zone. For many Black, indigenous, and people of color (BIPOC), this book may bring up some of the trauma and pain you may have experienced around race and racism. You don't have to face these questions alone, join the movement at www.awakenedlovewarrior.com.

Sharing your thoughts and experiences has the power to heal you and create profound connection to others, and it may have a transformative impact on someone else's life. Tag me or privately message me @iamsoniaroberts and #WhiteAlly to share your experience online. Important: please be mindful about what you post so you do not harm or trigger others.

Throughout the book, I will share some of my personal experiences around racism. While these instances are extremely painful, this book is about the bigger picture of systemic racism. It is about tying individual instances of racism to the structural changes that are required in order to achieve racial justice.

Thank you, I have deep gratitude that you are here, slowly turning the pages and deeply reflecting on who you are and race.

1 Ahimsa ~ Nonviolence

The "N" Word

When I was about seven years old, I was walking home from school, when the paper boy rode by and called me a "Nigger." I looked up and froze, standing like a statue on the sidewalk in front of my house. I stopped breathing. I couldn't speak. Finally when my legs could move, I ran inside and told my father what happened. I told him it was the paper boy who lived up the street. My father was livid; he immediately went to the paper boy's house and talked to his parents. They said their son would never use that word. My father cancelled the newspaper.

This incident brought me great pain and even today, writing about it brings up so much emotion. My world changed forever that day. This was the day I lost my innocence. I was scared. I felt small. I understood that people viewed me as more than different, as less than. I understood what it meant to have black skin in a world that tells you white skin is better. I no longer felt safe in my own skin, nor in my neighborhood, nor in my own home. Up until that day, I had run around our yard as a carefree child. My freedom was stolen from me that day. That one word, those 5 seconds, changed my life forever.

"Once we drop fear, we can draw nearer to people, we can draw nearer to the earth, we can draw nearer to all the heavenly creatures that surround us." ~bell hooks

The first Yama or guideline is Ahimsa, a Sanskrit word that means nonviolence or non-harming. Non-harming to yourself, to other people or to the planet. This is not limited to your actions but begins with your thoughts and your words. Ahimsa is also the absence of injustice, violence and cruelty. Practice kindness and compassion for yourself, every living being and our planet. Learn to be loving to yourself in your thoughts, words and actions.

Practicing nonviolence may seem passive, unimportant or obvious. Of course, you should not kill people or do physical harm to others. Unfortunately, the world has a long history of violence against others. America has a history of doing harm through 250 years of slavery, segregation, mass incarceration, near genocide of Native Americans, inequality for women, internment of Japanese Americans and more.

Ahimsa is about understanding privilege, power and oppression. It guides you to understand and recognize the imbalance of power in our country, as well as the world. It is critical to understand the power and privilege you possess or lack, as you practice, teach and share yoga. Now is the time to wake up and have a real conversation about race, oppression, white supremacy, and privilege. Are you willing to show up to the conversation? And if you are white, are you willing to understand and name your whiteness as you examine your power and privilege? A deepened yoga practice urges you to examine inequities between men and women, gay and straight, black and white, young and old, Christian and Muslim, and recognize that racism, sexism, classism, and phobias based on gender and sexual identity exist. Be sensitive to the fact that people are getting hurt, and just because it may not be happening to you directly, doesn't mean it's not happening. Are you complicit in the suffering of the world?

> "It is in the intelligent self-interest of white Americans to challenge racism, knowing they will not be free of sexism, class bias, homophobia, and ethnocentrism until black people are free of racism." ~Ibram X Kendi

Privilege, Power and Oppression

We must do the work of examining systems of power, privilege and oppression on our pathway to compassionate action and loving kindness. It is critical that you begin this journey with an understanding of the following terms:

Oppression is the subjugation of one group of people to elevate another group of people. It can include physical, emotional, mental, and spiritual violence. Oppression includes all the "isms," such as racism, sexism, elitism, ageism, heterosexism, classism, colorism, and ableism. You can have all the right beliefs about social equality and still practice oppression.

Internalized oppression is when members of oppressed or marginalized groups hold an oppressive view toward their own group, or they start to affirm negative stereotypes of themselves. The person may feel a sense of inferiority.

Colorism is discrimination based on skin color. Darker skinned people are treated worse than lighter skin people by whites or members of their own race.

Privilege is the benefit bestowed on people socially, politically and economically, based on a hierarchical ideal of race, class, age, ability level, mental health status, religion, language, gender identity, sex and even body type. A set of advantages that you have and others do not.

White privilege is the societal privilege that benefits white people over non-white people. It does not mean you have never struggled or worked hard to achieve success. White privilege does not always come with affluence. Being privileged does not necessarily mean that you have a perfect life. It does not mean that you come from wealth or that you always obtain everything you want or deserve. White privilege means that you were born with an inherent advantage over every other race of people.

White supremacy is a racist ideology based upon the belief that white people are superior to people of other races and therefore white people should be dominant over other races by social, political, and economic means. Whiteness and white supremacy were invented to justify slavery and other forms of exploitation.

Race is a socially constructed category of identification based on physical characteristics, created by man, not by nature. Race is not scientifically or biologically real, yet it's very real politically and socially. The DNA of all human beings is 99.9% alike.[4]

Racism is the belief in the superiority of one race over another, which often results in discrimination and prejudice towards people based on their race or ethnicity. Race hate groups began growing with the election of Barack Obama and have spiked since the beginning of Donald Trump's presidential campaign. Hate crimes have been on the rise not just in the United States, but all over the world.[5] White supremacists have been emboldened. Xenophobia and anti-immigration rhetoric has intensified. These are examples of prejudice, bias and hate, but systemic racism is something different.

Systemic racism is racism that infects the very structure of our society. Systemic racism persists in our schools, offices, court system, police departments, military and elsewhere. White people occupy most positions of decision-making power so people of color have a difficult time achieving social and political equality. For example, reducing racist police behavior to a few bad cops who need to be removed, rather than seeing it exists in police departments all over the United States, neglects the systemic cause. Even when Black athletes, such as former NFL player Colin Kaepernick, peacefully protest, there is a

---

[4] According to National Human Genome Research Institute.

[5] According to a study conducted by Carlo Schwarz and Karsten Muller, researchers at U.K.'s University of Warwick.

refusal to see police brutality as part of a system, and that the system needs to change.

Institutionalized racism is a form of racism expressed in the practice of social and political institutions. It is a pattern of differential access to material resources and power by race, which advantages one sector of the population while disadvantaging another. It's not only about racist attitudes or prejudice, but the ways in which rights and resources are distributed. Institutionalized racism disrupts marginalized communities' access to quality education, healthcare, living wages, a respectable quality of living and other resources. For example, in Michigan, the Flint water, racial and poverty crisis allowed contaminated water into Flint homes for years and still counting. Politicians knowingly poisoned black and brown children in Flint Michigan because "profits reign supreme."

Racism = Social + Institutional Power + Race Prejudice

Microaggressions[6] are "brief and commonplace daily verbal, behavioral, or environmental indignities, whether intentional or unintentional, that communicate hostile, derogatory, or negative racial slights and insults toward people of color." A few examples: Asking the following questions, "What are you?" Or, "What are you mixed with?" Or saying, "You don't act like a normal Black person." "I never see you as a Black girl." "You're really pretty for a Black girl." "Why do you sound white?" "That is so ghetto." Or "You don't sound Black." Racial profiling is a microaggression. Racism is not only in extremes, such as the white

---

[6] Dr. Chester Pierce coined the term microaggressions in 1970.

hoods of the Ku Klux Klan; microaggressions are more prevalent in everyday racism. Microaggressions are racial bias.

Racial bias is a racist belief. Racial bias, whether conscious or unconscious, often results in discrimination. Racism is what happens when that belief becomes an action. For example, a police officer shoots an unarmed black person because he "feared for his life."

Ally is a person whose commitment to dismantling oppression is reflected in a willingness to do the following: educate oneself about oppression; learn from and listen to people who are targets of oppression; examine and challenge one's own prejudices and assumptions; work through feelings of guilt, shame, and defensiveness to understand what is beneath them and what needs to be healed; learn and practice the skills of challenging oppressive remarks, behaviors, policies, and institutional structures; act collaboratively with members of the target group to dismantle oppression.[7]

"I believe that this nation can only heal from the wounds of racism if we all begin to love blackness. And by that I don't mean that we love only that which is best within us, but that we're also able to love that which is faltering, which is wounded, which is contradictory, incomplete." ~bell hooks

---

[7] According to Vanderbilt.edu

America's Birth Defect

There continues to be a widening racial wealth gap. It's probably unrealistic to believe that everything could be equally divided. But we can transform our systems in ways that will re-distribute rights and resources amongst all races more equally. It is possible to create a greater sense of reciprocity in the United States and in the world.

Racism is woven into the fabric of our society, so much so that many white people are unaware of the impact of racism. Unfortunately, whiteness and white privilege are often invisible to white people. White people have significant political, economic, and social power. If racial equality is to be achieved, it will require white recognition that racism continues today. Undoing whiteness and white supremacy begins with *you*.

White parents play an important role in facilitating racial change. Parents have to stop teaching white children that everyone is the same. Instead, openly discuss embracing differences. A simple act, to begin to create change, could start with a necessary and important conversation about how racism still exists today. White people aren't outside of race; they are at the top of the racial hierarchy.

Institutionalized racism is America's birth defect. It's important to acknowledge the emotions you might feel of denial, grief or anger. Accept your feelings and then transform that pain and suffering into something beautiful: a country that lives up to the promise of liberty and justice for all. Institutionalized racism has yet to be transformed, but it can be once we are ready to be honest and take the first step toward redemptive conversations, deep healing, true confessions and reparations. Without acknowledging this problem, we can never move past it. Racism will be the demise of this country if we don't deal with it.

"In a racist society, it is not enough to be non-racist — we must be anti-racist." ~Angela Davis

Active AntiRacist

What does it mean to be a more active anti-racist?

Anti-racism is an active way of seeing and being in the world in order to transform it. It's not enough to be a nice, good, non-racist. It's a process of creating another way to be white. It's learning to be white without seeing white as the norm.

The work always begins with yourself, moves to your immediate community, and then out to the world. Begin with difficult but impactful conversations. Call in or call out your friends and family on racist stereotypes. Explore how to affect decision-makers to create a more human and less hostile world for Black and other marginalized people in America and throughout the world. Challenge racism and uplift the Black community, or any marginalized community, by being an ethical and decent person who uses your voice to speak up against injustices. Strive to be allies with Black anti-racist leaders, support anti-racist activists and organizations. When you see injustice, don't be a non-racist bystander. Be actively anti-racist.

Learn to recognize and understand your own privilege. This is one of the first steps to eliminating racial discrimination. Educate yourself about oppression. Learn from and listen closely to people who are targets of oppression. Engage in tough conversations about race and injustice. We can no longer be afraid to discuss oppression and discrimination for fear of "getting it wrong." Ask questions so you gain understanding.

I don't think I have a racist bone in my body?

Racism is insidious. We are born into a racist society. It informs your thoughts, words, and actions.

"Love is an action." ~bell hooks

Love In Action

Love in action begins with how you treat yourself. Self-love or becoming inwardly loving to all parts of yourself is critical in expressing love, kindness and compassion toward others. The ability to see all of yourself, both the divinity and the imperfections, with complete acceptance leads to a loving, forgiving, open heart and mind. Non-harming others begins with loving yourself completely. There is often so much focus on changing, judging or fixing yourself, rather than on loving yourself. Take the time to explore the things you do not love about yourself. Examine how you speak to yourself, it matters. Learn to accept your full self and let go of harsh judgements, comparison to others and self-hatred.

It takes courage to take full responsibility for your thoughts, words, and actions. When you do find the courage to face your fears and love yourself fully and completely, you learn compassion and gain the ability to clearly see real love, just as it is. Real love is unconditional love without expectations or limitations, allowing yourself and others to be open, honest and free.

As your vision grows larger than your story and your personal version of the world, you can move past your own individual experience and into a larger consciousness about our collective culture. Love in action invites you to become more fully yourself, as you allow others to do the same.

> *"Your task is not to seek for love, but merely to seek and find all the barriers within yourself that you have built against it."~Rumi*

Ahimsa, nonviolence, asks you to open your heart and mind, to do no harm, to recognize your power and privilege, and to respect the relationship you have with yourself, others and the planet.

Heart Chakra Meditation: Awakening to Suffering

Sit or lie down in a comfortable position
Close your eyes or soften your gaze
Draw a deep cleansing breath into your heart
And exhale through your mouth

Now allow gentle, easy breaths through your nose
As you are breathing, notice the rise and fall of your chest
Begin to breathe full and complete breaths through your nose,
into your heart center
Exhale slowly through your nose
Full and complete breaths into your heart center
Exhale all the way out

Notice your own suffering
Notice how it manifests in your body and emotions
Hold compassion in your heart
Release suffering with each breath
Return to awareness of full and complete breaths

Notice suffering of marginalized and oppressed people
Feel the suffering in your body and emotions
Hold compassion in your heart
Release suffering with each breath

Notice suffering of privileged people
Feel the guilt, defensiveness, and disconnection

Feel this energy in your body and emotions
Hold compassion in your heart
Release suffering with each breath

Go deeper into the body
Into the heart
As you breathe
Imagine pure light radiating from your heart

Fills you with glowing love
Infinite love
Spreads throughout your entire body
Into the Universe

Know you are an Infinite Being of Light
You are Divine Love
Sense your body and your breath
Sense pure light at your heart center

Return to easy gentle breaths through the nose
When you are ready, open your eyes

Namaste, and so it is

Ahimsa ~ Nonviolence Reflection Questions

1. What are some ways you see oppression and privilege in your daily life? Can you identify ways in which you may be perpetuating or colluding with racism? How can this be changed?

2. Have you witnessed systemic or institutional racism? If so, write about it. If not, see if you can awaken to it this coming week.

3. Examine and challenge your own biases, prejudices and conditioning. Identify any bias you have or beliefs/conditioning you may need to let go of. Work through feelings of guilt, shame, and defensiveness to understand what is beneath them and what needs to be healed.

4. How do you feel about yourself? Do you love yourself? Are you accepting or critical of yourself and/or others?

2 Satya ~ Truthfulness

"Your silence will not protect you." ~Audre Lorde

T he second Yama or guideline is Satya, a Sanskrit word that means truth. It means to be truthful in one's thoughts, words, and actions. Satya means staying true to yourself, your faith, and your life while constantly seeking the truth. You follow integrity and compassion to find the truth. It also means learning to speak your truth without causing harm (ahimsa) to yourself or to anyone emotionally, mentally or spiritually. However, living and speaking your truth may cause others discomfort. This discomfort provides an opportunity for one to reflect on their words, actions and/or belief system.

Satya encourages you to live your truth and see the truth, over feeling a sense of belonging or fitting in. When you are the person who stands up against bullies, or defends people who are being made fun of, or when you are the person who becomes an ally to the oppressed, you are practicing satya, or truthfulness. Strive to develop a new norm centered on truthfulness.

Stand Up and Speak Out

"A man who stands for nothing will fall for anything." ~Malcolm X

Satya is having the courage to stand up and speak out against injustices in the world. We live in a culture where fear rules the world. People are motivated, manipulated and driven by fear. Fear creates violence. Fear-based anger is the primary motive for violence. Learn to mindfully sit with your anger. Don't resist; allow and listen to it. Often, underneath anger, we will find fear. Anger provides a surge of energy, while fear leaves us feeling vulnerable or helpless. Learn to mindfully sit with your fear. Don't resist; allow and listen to it.

In order to sit with your anger and fear, then to speak up compassionately and stand up for yourself and others, you need to have courage. You will need to be vulnerable. The more you practice stepping out of your comfort zone, the more your courage will grow. As you gain confidence, you will find more ease in speaking your truth.

Practice satya with the intention to positively influence the environment and society that surrounds you. It's not about being fearless; it's about cultivating the courage to face your fears. Just like ahimsa, non-violence, it takes great courage to practice satya, truthfulness.

Ancestral Roots

One day, I was telling a white father that I would love to live in Hawaii. He told me about a time when he lived there and how it was hard for him and a friend to get jobs there. He shared with me how

Native Hawaiians were "not too fond of the white man." His friend ended up having to work at Starbucks.

Native Hawaiians have good reason to resent white people. America destroyed the kingdom of Hawaii.[8] Hawaii faced continual denigration of its beliefs and practices by missionaries and other white supremacist ideas. It is very important to know the history of the land you are on. But what his comment brought up for me is, that is exactly how Black people feel in the United States. And here he was seemingly unaware talking to me, a Black woman, about experiencing discrimination. I was going to ease into sharing this insight with him. I decided to start by telling him, "My grandmother, Juana Lopez, was born in Hilo, Hawaii, in 1914." Unfortunately, that was all I was able to share with him because he seemed uncomfortable and walked away. In the United States, African Americans continue to experience job discrimination,[9] redlining,[10] gentrification,[11] predatory lending and more.

Think about your ancestral roots. When you are talking to people of color, consider their ancestral roots. For African Americans, our ancestors were stolen from their land, enslaved, separated from their

[8] According to history.com, in January 1893, a revolutionary "Committee of Safety," organized by Sanford B. Dole, staged a coup against Queen Liliuokalani with the tacit support of the United States.

[9] In 2017, Harvard University Business School Review documented that hiring discrimination against African Americans was still a reality and did not decline in the past 25 years.

[10] Redlining is an unlawful discriminatory practice whereby mortgage lenders draw red lines around Black neighborhoods on a map indicating areas in which they do not want to make loans.

[11] Gentrification leads to negative impacts such as forced displacement, promoting discriminatory behavior by people of power and a focus on spaces that exclude low-income individuals and people of color.

families, sold, beaten, whipped, lynched, raped, terrorized, falsely accused of crimes, incarcerated and killed by white people. These atrocities continued post-slavery and we never received reparations. The slavery system in the United States was a national system that helped build a world economy.[12]

Being Your True Self

Being your true self takes boldness and may not always be comfortable for others. As scary as it can be, you have to make the choice to speak your truth. By facing your fears and stepping out of your comfort zone, you step closer to living your truth. In asana (posture) practice, people love practicing the poses they have mastered or poses that come easy to them. You resist or even avoid the asanas that may greatly benefit you because they are challenging or make you uncomfortable. I'm not talking about advanced postures that may or may not be attainable, but even the simplest posture, such as savasana/corpse pose, is often uncomfortable and avoided by many people. More often, sitting still and simple breathing is the most challenging and uncomfortable posture for practitioners. There is no way to run or avoid, move or distract yourself. You have to sit and face yourself, your fears, your hopes, your dreams, your disappointments, your limitations, your privilege, and your disadvantage, and simply see them, feel them and be with them. Learn to be still, be present, and allow everything to just be what it is.

---

[12] According to Jubilee: The Emergence of African American Culture by the Schomburg Center for Research in Black Culture of the New York Public Library.

"The truth will set you free, but first it will piss you off." ~Gloria Steinem

Tell Me Where To Grow

Satya, truthfulness, is like saying to a trusted friend, "Tell me about myself." Be willing to look at the truth of who you are and surround yourself with people who will tell you the truth about yourself, with love and compassion. You need to face the truth in order to grow. You need to face the truth so you can become the best version of yourself. Can you receive the truth, the positive and the criticism, in a loving way?

The pathway to healing is being honest and calling out or naming whatever the truth is, especially injustices. If it is racism, say it. If it is sexism, say it. If it is homophobia, say it. Speak up. Stand up. If someone calls it out in you, be willing to receive it. Can you receive feedback about your racist language or behavior without becoming defensive or shutting down?

Code Switching

Satya or truthfulness includes code switching or language alteration for many Black, indigenous, people of color (BIPOC).

"It is a peculiar sensation, this double-consciousness, this sense of always looking at one's self through the eyes of others...One ever feels his twoness, -the American, a Negro; two souls, two thoughts, two unreconciled strivings, two warring ideals in one dark body, whose dogged strength alone keeps it from being torn asunder." ~Dr. W.E.B Du Bois

Double consciousness is a concept that Dr. W.E.B. Du Bois introduced in his book The Souls of Black Folk, written in 1903. Double consciousness is the feeling that you have more than one social identity, which makes it difficult to develop a sense of self. As African Americans, we are forced to view ourselves from the perspective of both cultures. This challenges our ability to unify our African American subculture with our American identity.

Code switching is an idea of authenticity, speaking with a voice that is true to you, that is real for you, but it becomes complicated when you have to navigate between different worlds. Often, it's not a conscious effort; it just happens.

People of color are constantly in the act of making those around them feel comfortable. Whether it is our looks, hair, dress, tone of voice, subtle actions or aggressive actions, we are commonly not accepted as our true self. Many BIPOC who work in the corporate world may use a voice that is considered a "white" sounding voice. However, when we are with our friends, we may use a more laid-back, "cool" sounding voice, like in the film Sorry to Bother You.[13]

Most people code switch, but people of color have to do it the most as a means of survival in a white dominated world. Privilege is being able to not have to think about the way you say and do things in every moment so you can relax and bloom into your true self.

---

[13] Sorry to Bother You is a 2018 American science-fiction dark comedy film written and directed by Boots Riley.

Acceptance

Accept the truth; when you do, a new door opens and you are able to expand and grow. You are awake, paying attention, and you can make the right choice or the best choice in the moment. Update your values, beliefs and views in order to become the best version of yourself. The truth of who you are is beyond a box and a label. There are no limits. See no limits in your life. There is indeed great power in the truth. There is great power in expressing your uniqueness and authenticity, and allowing others to do the same. Focus on accepting yourself and accepting others, just as they are. See limitless possibilities, real love and nothing but the truth.

Satya, truthfulness, encourages you to become your true authentic self and asks you to look at the truth of who you are, the truth of your impact on those around you, and the truth of the world.

Self-Expression Meditation: Connecting with YourAuthentic Self

Sit or lie down in a comfortable position
Close your eyes or soften your gaze
Draw a deep cleansing breath into your nose
And exhale through your mouth

Now allow gentle, easy breaths through your nose
As you are breathing, notice the rise and fall of your belly
Notice the rise and fall of your heart center or chest
Begin to breathe full and complete breaths in through your nose
Exhale slowly through your nose
Full and complete breaths in
Exhale all the way out

Arrive fully in the moment
Slow down and lengthen the breath
Become quieter and quieter, still, open

Move your awareness to your heart
Sense the beating of your heart
Connect to your heart's energy, power, vibration
Relax into your heartbeat

From the space of your heart
Observe the way you are living your life right now
Allow yourself to see clearly

Who you are
Who you are with others
How do you wish to express yourself
Connect with your creative power
A power that radiates from your heart center

How does it feel when you do express yourself
When you speak your truth
When you stand up for yourself
When you stand up for others

Release all your fears
Release all your fears that you can't express yourself
All the fears that say you will not be accepted

Be willing to express your true self
However you choose
In all areas of your life

Allow the self-expression of your being
Not being bound by any label, any image, any box
By any thought, conditioning, or belief

Not binding others with limited thoughts or beliefs
Accept yourself, just as you are
Accept others, just as they are
See no limits

Allow yourself to be relaxed

Calm, content, open
Slowly uncovering who you are
And who you wish to be
What you wish to create
From moment to moment

Return your focus to the sensation of your breath
moving through your nose

When you are ready, slowly open your eyes

Namaste, and so it is

Satya ~ Truthfulness Reflection Questions

1. Write about a time when you practiced speaking your truth or spoke up against injustices. What was the outcome?

2. Are you silencing yourself or distorting yourself for others? If so, how and why?

3. Have you ever been called racist? If yes, how did you react?

4. Examine your beliefs and conditioning? Does this belief system yield compassion for the truth of yourself and others? What can you do to condition your thoughts, words and actions to move toward a more authentic you?

3 Asteya ~ Nonstealing

"It's so clear that you have to cherish everyone. I think that's what I get from these older black women, that sense that every soul is to be cherished, that every flower is to bloom. That is a very different world view from what we've been languishing under, where the thought is that the only way I can bloom is if I step on your flower, the only way I can shine is if I put out your light." ~Alice Walker

The third Yama or yoga guideline is Asteya, a Sanskrit word that means non-stealing. Consider all the things you can steal without even realizing or being aware. You can steal someone's time, shine, energy or culture. You can steal from the earth. You can even steal from yourself. Asteya means to reevaluate your words, thoughts and actions and course correct your behavior when needed. Asteya, non-stealing, reminds you to not steal from yourself, others or the planet.

Act of Erasing

For people of color, our life experiences are often shaped by the internalization of negative stereotypes and prejudices. Negative stereotypes perpetuated by the mainstream culture damage our sense of self. Stereotypes encourage doubt, self-criticism and inhibitions. Both my grandparents and parents struggled to integrate American culture without losing, rejecting or erasing their country of origin. The history of oppression has a way of erasing people, cultures, religions and traditions.

I grew up in a very self-critical family. My grandfather drove around in a car with a license plate that read, "El Feo," or the ugly. He thought being self-deprecating would be attractive to women. I am slowly breaking free from that way of thinking. Hopefully, I'm breaking the cycle for my own children. Don't "steal" your own shine by diminishing your self-worth. Practice love, kindness and acceptance of self and others.

When I met my husband, I thought it was crazy and conceited the way he would look in the mirror and say positive things to himself and kiss himself on the shoulders. That is not the way I was raised. He taught our son and daughter to look at themselves in the mirror and say, "I look shaaaarp. Today is going to be a great day." He is always expecting the best possible outcome, and I am often preparing for the worst.

One of the most powerful experiences I've had, was hearing my husband tell his friend how proud he was of him. I witnessed a grown Black man tell another grown Black man, "I am proud of you," and I could hear the genuine excitement in his voice. Sadly, I never witnessed this before between men. It blew me away. This tenderness, pride and freedom from traditional ideas about gender was something I had never witnessed. Look for opportunities to lift people up. See the good in yourself and be willing to recognize and celebrate it in others.

"We have to consciously study how to be tender with each other until it becomes a habit because what was native has been stolen from us, the love of Black women for each other."
~Audre Lorde

Waking Up to Whiteness

White entitlement is acquired at birth by those with white skin. It begins with America being stolen from the Native Americans, followed by the enslavement of Africans, then Jim Crow laws that enforced racial segregation and mass incarceration. Mass lynchings[14] were allowed on this great land due to white entitlement.

Race and whiteness were not created by nature, but by man. These ideologies were made for reasons that had entirely to do with greed. Whiteness and white supremacy were invented to justify slavery and other forms of exploitation. The roots of white supremacy lie in establishing economic exploitation by the theft of resources and human labor.

White Americans have enjoyed entitlements for so long that many see it as deserving and something given to them by their forefathers. White entitlement is not new. This is American history.

---

[14] According to The National Memorial for Peace and Justice, More than 4400 African American men, women, and children were hanged, burned alive, shot, drowned, and beaten to death by white mobs between 1877 and 1950.

How do we wake up silent, apathetic, entitled white people in the yoga community and in the world? How do we wake up those who call themselves progressives as they point to other racist white people instead of looking at themselves?

This guideline is a reminder to cherish everyone. It is a reminder to act from a place of abundance, not greed or scarcity. Can we shift this paradigm?

Cultural Appropriation

"Acknowledging the good that you already have in your life is the foundation for all abundance." ~Eckhart Tolle, A New Earth

Asteya reminds you to appreciate not appropriate. Appropriation is the action of taking something for one's own use, typically without the owner's permission. Cultural appropriation is the adoption of the elements of the originating, minority culture by members of the dominant culture. There is an imbalance of power present. Often, the adoption of these cultural elements is for profit.

Cultural appropriation is when someone thinks the art or practice of a culture is cool but not the people from whom it originates. You love the culture, but not the people. This is evidenced by the disrespect, disregard, distortion, and even the failure to pay homage to the originating, minority culture. You may have seen yogis wear bindis, by placing sticky sparkles at the center of their forehead. Words like "tribe" and "gypsy" can be offensive, often misused and printed on t-shirts for profit. These are examples of cultural appropriation. When Black hairstyles like bantu knots, dreadlocks and corn rows ("boxer braids") are labeled as "ghetto" or "unprofessional" on a Black person, but seen as trendy and cool on a non-Black person; that is cultural appropriation.

African American Vernacular English, or AAVE, is appropriated by white people, non-Black people of color, and companies daily. Using words like, *lit, bae, woke,* and many more phrases can be traced back to AAVE. When companies, white people, or non-Black people of color use it, they are co-opting its cool potential for their own (financial) gain and typically don't give anything back to the community that created it.

I have been harmed several times by a non-Black yoga teacher of color that loves to use AAVE but continually posts anti-Black sentiments on social media. Be mindful of the authenticity of the language you use, where the language comes from and the potential harm of your social media posts. Words have power and they can cause harm. As long as Black people are still oppressed, the usage of our vernacular by white people and companies will always have a harmful affect.

It is essential to respect and acknowledge different cultures and traditions and to be aware of your actions. Love the world, appreciate, and respect all people, cultures, traditions and religions. In many cases, it is not only about your race, but it is about your intention, as well as your impact.

One way to avoid appropriating is to educate yourself on the culture and tradition. Learn the history and give credit to who or what inspired you. Cultural exchange can be a beautiful practice, as long as you are paying homage to the originating culture. If you are unsure, you can ask yourself, will this make someone uncomfortable? Is it harmful/ ahimsa? And is what I am doing or saying authentic, satya, truthful to me? If there is a possibility that someone somewhere could be even slightly offended by your consumption of their cultural practice, then don't do it.

Where is the line between appreciating and appropriating?

It's important to continue to heighten your awareness of power imbalances that have resulted from colonialism and oppression. It's a meaningful and continuous conversation. Ask yourself, do I have their consent?

Focus on your creativity and avoid stealing from others. Identify your skills and abilities. Innovative ideas are a result of careful study and authenticity. Create your own cultural identifiers.

Acknowledge Power, Privilege and Impact

"Blossom your buttocks, like an African dancer," instructed the white yoga teacher trainer, as I stood in one of my first yoga teacher trainings. The yoga students rotated their inner thighs back, and stuck out their butts. I was in a classroom of 30 students, mostly white women and no other Black students. When I heard this instruction, I froze and stopped breathing. I was in shock. I could not speak.

Later that day, I sent an email to the yoga teacher trainer, let's call her "T" for simplicity, explaining that I found her words inappropriate, harmful and racially offensive. After receiving my email, T called me, we attempted a conversation, but T could not understand how her language was offensive and racist. I explained, for comparison, that one would not say, "Flatten your buttocks like a European dancer." T still could not understand and refused to listen carefully as I explained why it was offensive. T informed me that this was an instruction learned from her senior teacher. (Many years later that senior teacher she referred to, was involved in a scandal and would eventually step down.) T could not understand and insisted that we discuss this with the entire class next time we met. This was happening, not because I wanted to discuss with the entire class, but because T wanted to. I knew I was going to be re-traumatized in the classroom. I was furious and incredibly hurt by the use of this racist stereotype and by T's refusal to apologize and recognize that what was said was hurtful and wrong.

Why couldn't T accept responsibility and apologize? How could T expect to have a conversation about how to go forward together? As a person of white privilege, T could never fully understand the ways in which oppressive acts or language impact Black people. However, T could certainly listen with intention to understand and work to change this behavior or language. A simple, yet revolutionary act, to begin to create change, could start with a sincere apology. Next, T could spend time reflecting on the harmful impact of her words and actions. Then, move forward acknowledging her power, privilege and accountability.

Intent vs Impact

At the next training, T asked the class, full of mostly white students, if anyone else was offended. Unsurprisingly, maybe two people raised their hands and the rest of the class looked confused. As if that wasn't degrading enough, then T led a passive-aggressive discussion and yoga practice about my perceived insecurity. My experience of T's racist instruction was dismissed and viewed as my insecurity about my African blossomed buttocks. But the thing is, I wish my buttocks were blossomed, like any dancer really! Please and thank you. I was not ashamed about being African American, or about blossomed buttocks; the point is that she offended me by using a racist stereotype in a yoga classroom full of mostly white women, except me. This is the exact opposite of cultural inclusivity.

The teacher, T, completely disrespected me and my African heritage, while the rest of the students acted like T was some kind of deity or enlightened being. You may be wondering why I didn't run out of that room and toxic situation and demand my money back! Unfortunately, situations like these are so common, you become use to them and they become the norm. I chose to complete the program to receive my yoga certification and endure the toxic environment. I've been aware of racism since I was seven years old, when the paperboy in my neighborhood called me the N word. Somehow, I still manage to feel shocked and speechless when I encounter racism and silent bystanders.

Creating a discussion about intent is inherently a privileged action. Jamie Utt writes, "It ensures that you and your identity (and intent) stay at the center of any conversation and action while the impact of your action or words on those around you is marginalized. So, if someone ever tells you to "check your privilege," what they may very well mean is: "Stop centering your experience and identity in the conversation by making this about the intent of your actions instead of their impact."

Unfortunately, people are often unconscious of their racial bias and their impact on others. People do things without realizing that their actions and words matter. You can choose your impact on others. If the impact of your actions is furthering oppression, then you need to pause, listen, reflect, and work to change the behavior. Practice being intentional about your impact. And do not force people of color into conversations about race.

White Silence

In Layla Saad's workbook[15] Me & White Supremacy, there is a chapter on white silence. "It is when people with white privilege stay complicitly silent when it comes to issues of race. White silence is how YOU stay silent around race."

Here is an excerpt from Layla Saad's workbook:

Why Do You Need to Look at White Silence?

Because silence is not neutral. Silence is looking the other way and protecting your privilege - thus continuing to uphold white supremacy. White silence is violence. White silence protects the system. White silence prevents you from speaking truth to power. You must look at the ways in which you stay silent, so that you can begin to build the strength and courage to start using your voice. As Audre Lorde said, "your silence will not protect you." When you stay silent, you stay complicit.

There was only one person in the room of yoga students who supported me. There was also a beautiful white woman who tried to connect with me by sharing that she has always been insecure about her thick things, implying that I am insecure about my "blossomed buttocks." The yoga teacher trainer, T, was able to rationalize her racist remarks since the yoga students didn't have a reaction, and I was seen as overreacting or insecure.

---

[15] www.meandwhitesupremacybook.com

This story is a perfect illustration of white silence. It also illustrates ahimsa, non-harming, satya, speaking your truth, and asteya, non-stealing. She stole something from me that day by stereotyping African bodies. Black and brown bodies are not safe in this society. Those who were silent were complicit in upholding racist behavior. White solidarity increased the racial divide rather than bridge our differences. The yoga teacher trainer, T, showed no concern for my feelings, no curiosity of my experience, nor did she really listen to why I took offense. T arrogantly remained confident that she was right and I was wrong.

Listen, Reflect, and Transform

When conversations of racism come up, instead of jumping into defense mode, which makes you unable to really hear and understand the pain and challenges of Black, indigenous, people of color (BIPOC), pause and listen carefully. Listen to understand, reflect and work to change the harmful behavior. Ask yourself, Am I trying to be right or am I trying to understand and be better?

Racism is deeply engrained in our society, and it impacts how we engage with each other daily. We must undo the view that only intentionally mean people can participate in racism. Be grateful when you are called out for racism, not defensive. It is a gift for you to learn a valuable lesson. It may be uncomfortable, but what you do next is what matters.

Asteya, nonstealing, reminds you to focus on your abundance and how you would like to authentically impact the world. It reminds you to acknowledge your power, privilege and impact. Appreciate, don't appropriate, as you identify and cultivate your skills and abilities. Save your toxic criticism, and deepen your love.

Knowing Your Worth Meditation: I Am Worthy

Sit or lie down in a comfortable position
Close your eyes or soften your gaze
Draw a deep cleansing breath in through your nose
And exhale through your mouth
Now breathe easy gentle breaths through the nose

Draw a full breath into your abdomen, pause, relax, breathe out
Relax your whole body
Be present
Be still
Open your heart
Open your mind

I am most certainly worthy of this time dedicated to my own
well-being

Be present
Be still
Open your heart
Open your mind

I am worthy of knowing my manifesting power
I am worthy of peace
I am worthy of happiness
I am worthy of deep connection and intimacy
I am worthy of feeling safe

I am worthy of seeing my own beauty

Draw a full breath in, pause, relax, exhale
Be present
Be still
Open your heart
Open your Mind

I am worthy of my overall well-being

Return to easy gentle breaths through the nose
Slowly open your eyes when you are ready

Namaste, and so it is

Asteya ~ Nonstealing Reflection Questions

1. Can you identify a time when you may have participated in cultural appropriation? Can you identify a time when you may have said or done something to offend someone else's culture? Write and reflect about it.

2. Write about something you can do to build a connection to a marginalized group or a less privileged community. How can you actively become an ally in a way that feels authentic and rewarding?

3. How might it feel to celebrate others? Celebrate yourself? Can you see the benefit of celebrating yourself/others? Are you ready to?

4 Brahmacharya ~ Nonexcess

The fourth Yama or yoga guideline is Brahmacharya, a Sanskrit word that means nonexcess. Do not allow feelings of lack or emptiness rule your world. Find a sacred balance by practicing brahmacharya, nonexcess, moderation and "right use of energy." Brahmacharya guides us to live and behave in a way that leads towards the Divine, God or Higher Power. Consider how you use and direct your energy. Direct your energy away from external desires and other people's business, and instead direct it towards finding lasting peace, joy and simplicity. The avoidance of excess or extremes, especially in our behavior, will lead to a more joyful life.

God's Plan

Following God's plan means moving in rhythm with God, moving in rhythm with the universe. Move in harmony, unity and faith on your journey to wholeness and healing. See God in yourself and see God in everything. All people. Cherish all people. Moving with the rhythm of life is like living inside the mantra, Om. Living inside the universal sound ohmmm.

Practice the yoga asanas or postures to create shapes with your body, space, flowing breath, and alignment. Can you stay connected and create that harmony off the mat? As you cultivate a deeper connection and awareness of yourself, can you then build a heightened awareness of the world around you? Can you heighten your awareness to the suffering of others? Can you move through the world with an open heart, an open mind, and a sense of wonder, curiosity and compassion?

Before you can connect with God, learn to let go of distractions that draw you away from God. If you become obsessed with other people's lives, busy-ness, work and earning money to the point of neglecting your values, like your family, your body and spirit, then you've allowed your obsessions to become a distraction from aligning with God and living authentically.

There was a time in my life when I was in a really dark place. I became obsessed with achieving things that may have looked impressive on the outside, but I wasn't doing anything that made me feel connected and fulfilled on the inside. During this time, I became increasingly unhappy and wasn't sure I wanted to live anymore. I thought I would only know peace by leaving this world. I used alcohol to numb myself, to avoid my feelings and to forget my pain. It was a long road of suffering. Slowly, I began to surround myself with people who lifted me up, and I used my dance training as a cathartic experience. Dance provided an emotional release for me. I would also go to a park to be outside, under a tree and in the sunshine. I needed to feel the sun on my skin and the harmony of nature. I needed to pause, be still and find a little peace.

When I found yoga, I knew I had to teach it. It helped me slow down, deeply connect to my breath and body, and sense inner peace. This mind-body integration led to experiencing a greater sense of vibrancy, well-being and joy. Sharing the many gifts of yoga with my students is a great honor, and it makes my heart full.

Intuition and Signs

Are you paying attention to the signs around you? Slow down. Listen and look with clear eyes. Look with the eyes of your heart. See where to go and sense what to do.

You have a blend of intuition and common sense that helps you live more skillfully. However, you have to be willing to listen, then act on your intuition. For example, your intuition will tell you who is interested in building a relationship and who will break your heart.

Everyone has a story. It is a story of pain, loss, grief, discovery and a story of adversity that is carried with them. Creating balance in your life means being honest with yourself about your story and how it has impacted you. Connect your personal story back to how you learned to be white. Then learn to discern between what is real and the story your mind is telling you. And that's all it really is: a story. Tap into your intuition. What is your intuition telling you about this story that is being played out?

"Everything in moderation, including moderation." ~Oscar Wilde

Strong and Fluid

Yoga builds your physical and mental strength. It helps you find the balance between ease and effort. Yoga is where strength and flexibility meet, and so it is in life. In yoga, there is a saying, sthira sukha, or steadiness and ease. You practice to find that sweet, sacred balance on your mat and beyond. Learn to find the balance of being strong and standing up for what you believe in, while being graceful and fluid to flow with the rhythm of life. Learn to meet people exactly where they are, and meet yourself exactly where you are. With life's twists, turns and challenges, can you remain strong and supple?

Listen to your body. Don't apologize for taking a break or resting. Rest when you need to; nap, or lie in savasana (corpse pose) the entire yoga class. Rest is vital for energizing and recharging your ability to show up fully for your community, colleagues, partner, children and yourself. It is impossible to be present and connected when you are exhausted. Rest. Reconnect. Recharge.

Mind Your Business/Racism

Brahmacharya reminds you to consider how you use and direct your energy. There is an old gospel song that says, "Sweep around your own front door before you try to sweep around mine."

Look carefully at whether or not you are using your power and privilege in ways that can intentionally hurt others. There is a lot of energy or intrusion into Black people simply living their everyday lives. You have most likely heard of "Permit Patty" or "BBQ Becky." There is a long list of white people calling the police on people of color, mostly

Black people, for the following: the Black Yale student in a common room on campus, a Black man waiting for his friend at Starbucks, a Black real estate investor inspecting a house he was interested in purchasing, a group of Black women staying in an Airbnb because they "did not wave," a Black firefighter in uniform and with proper identification, and the list goes on.

Who is "Permit Patty" and "BBQ Becky?"

Alison Ettel, also known as Permit Patty, called the police on an 8-year old Black girl selling water on a sidewalk in San Francisco, California. The little girl was trying to save up money to go to Disneyland.

BBQ Becky is a woman who called the police on two Black men grilling without a permit at Lake Merritt in Oakland, California.

We know that weaponizing the police against people of color for something that one personally does not like often results in death. Are you allowing Black people to take up space? Let Black people breathe, move and have some joy.

Sacred Balance

The body is sacred, as is all life. Focus on things that matter, that are sustainable, and that will give you lasting fulfillment. How much energy, time and money are you wasting on other people's business? Are your daily actions draining you of your vitality? Stop doing things that suck the life out of you and jeopardize the life of others. Free up your time and energy to be used for YOUR spiritual journey. Look for joy, look for peace and look for simplicity. Allow yourself space to pause and be still. Allow yourself space to breathe fully and completely. Allow your prana and vital energy to be freed up, to allow you to stay open, loving, and present. This is a guideline to not only mind your business, but to mind your racism, your conscious and unconscious biases, and privilege.

What do you mean mind your racism? I don't think I am racist.

According to John Dovidio, PhD, a professor of psychology and public health at Yale University, most white Americans have unconscious, implicit, racial biases. The majority of white Americans have bias because they've grown up in a culture that has been historically racist in many ways and they're exposed to the media that associates violence, drugs and poverty with certain groups.

Most people want to be considered good, moral people, which becomes the biggest obstacle to identifying your biases. So, you need to work at always being awake and receptive to the possibility that you might be biased. Do you want to look like a good person or do you want to practice being a good person?

What do you hold sacred?

"Your Lower Self asks, what's in it for me? Your Higher Self asks, how can I serve?" ~Father Richard Rohr

Focusing on your abundance and gratitude builds a bridge directly to your God. Meditation can help you clear your mind of distractions and bring you closer to God. Listening to life-affirming music, spending time at the ocean, enjoying the mountains, and being in nature can as well. Walk with other like-minded beings, who are on the same path. Surround yourself with people who are also on this awakening journey to wholeness. Take time to sit down, write and reflect about where you are, right now, in this moment, on your life journey. Walk. Rest. Be still, reflect, stumble, fall, get up and continue walking.

Brahmacharya, nonexcess, reminds you to let go of distractions, and excess, and instead to rest and recharge. Focus your energy and efforts to align with fairness, equality, justice and the Divine.

Soul Healing Meditation: Restoring Sacred Balance

Sit or lie down in a comfortable position
Close your eyes or soften your gaze
Draw a deep cleansing breath in through your nose
And exhale through your mouth
Now breathe easy gentle breaths through the nose
Drop into awareness of your body

Draw a full breath in to your heart center, pause, relax, breathe out
Notice the sensations in your body
More and more arrive fully and completely in the now
Ground and center yourself

Drop into the earth
Feeling embraced and supported
Silently say, "I feel balanced and aligned"

Rub your hands together briskly
Place your hands on your thighs
Grounding your body
Take several full and complete breaths

Rub your hands together briskly
Now place your hands one on top of the other
and gently press them against your heart center
Breathe full and complete breaths

Rub your hands together briskly
Place your hands one on top of the other
and gently press them against your solar plexus or upper abdomen
Inhale, expand your abdomen, pause, exhale,
gently contract your abdomen, pause
Inhale, expand your abdomen, pause, exhale,
gently contract your abdomen, pause

Silently say, "I am directing my energy inward
My heart is open and loving
My daily actions are for the collective good of all people
I look for joy
I look for peace
I look for simplicity

I am open and loving
My energy flows freely"

Draw a deep cleansing breath in through your nose
And exhale through your mouth
Relax your arms and hands

When you are ready, slowly open your eyes

Namaste, and so it is

Brahmacharya ~ Nonexcess Reflection Questions

1.You are a sacred being. In what ways can you honor yourself as sacred? What can you do to see the sacred in all?

2.How are you using your time and energy? Do you find yourself focused on the lives of others, while avoiding your own?

3.Have you experienced God or a higher power lately? What were you doing...meditating, praying, hiking, singing?

5 Aparigraha ~ Nonpossessiveness

"You alone are enough. You have nothing to prove to anybody."
~Maya Angelou

The fifth Yama or yoga guideline is Aparigraha, a Sanskrit word that means nonpossessiveness, non-grasping or non-greediness. This guideline encourages you to keep your desire for possessions to what is necessary or important. It reminds you to take only what you need, keep only what serves you in the moment and let go when the time is right. When you learn to let go and live without attachment, you experience freedom. This does not mean you do not set goals or aspire to greatness, but instead of grasping and clinging, you let go, stay open and find ways to nurture and center yourself so you feel strong and independent. Find ways to attain lasting happiness without requiring instant gratification or possessions.

Be Unattached

Be clear on what you want, and on the feelings that you want to experience every day: freedom, meaning, and purpose, and be unattached to how it comes to you. Practice generosity without attachment to recognition. Work for the love of it and not for the rewards. Avoid obsessing over an outcome, and instead, be willing to allow, receive, be present and trust in the Universe.

Your expectations often lead to disappointment. The more you cling to something, grasp and hold on too tightly, the more you block your own breath, energy flow and growth. You are blocking your own blessings. You are getting in your own way. When you become fixated on something, someone, or your feelings, you are not allowing abundance and opportunity to show up in your life. Allow greatness to come to you. Can you trust that there is something greater than you have ever imagined steadily making its way into your life?

Life's Rhythm: Receive and Release

Life is full of moments. You can live in the moment, and experience the moment, but you cannot stay there forever. The more you try to hold on, the more you experience discomfort and dis-ease. The only thing that is constant in your life is change. You cannot hold onto something that isn't yours to keep forever. Your children will grow up, your parents will grow old, your job will undoubtedly change or end, your role in your marriage or relationship will change. You cannot possess your children or your partners. There is a rhythm to live by, receive and release, inhale and exhale, expand and contract. Be willing to trust. Trust the Universe, but more importantly, trust yourself.

> *"If you love something, let it go. If it returns, it's yours; if it doesn't, it wasn't. If you love someone, set them free. If they come back, they're yours; if they don't, they never were."*
> *~Richard Bach*

Before I married my husband, we called off the wedding and separated. I had to walk away. I was willing to walk away and break my own heart because I loved, valued and respected myself. It was one of the hardest and most painful things I've had to do. I still loved him and cared for him deeply, but I had to let go. I could not allow myself to cling or grasp onto something that was no longer real. Someone asked me, "Is it a yes, or is it a no?" It was definitely a no. He was not ready. We were not ready.

It was a scary time for me because I had changed my whole life to make this relationship work, and by choosing to walk away, it felt as though I had nothing. At the time, I had no car, no job, and nowhere to live. I could've easily stayed to avoid this low point of my life, but I knew I had to leave. So, I left.

We ended up getting married about a year later, but first, we spent time apart. Then we worked on our relationship and built a stronger foundation. I eventually moved in with him again and then, I asked him to marry me. Now we have two beautiful children and twelve years (and counting) of a marriage full of lessons, blessings, personal and spiritual growth, deep connection and unconditional love.

How many emotional bags are you carrying?

Like Erykah Badu sings, "pack light" while moving through the journey of life. You are going to hurt your back, your body, and your whole self, carrying around expectations, resentments and unforgiven moments. It is not easy to care deeply and enjoy every moment to its fullest and then let it go. It is not easy to let go and forgive those who have caused you pain. Often, you don't want to let go for fear of losing something, but if you don't let go, you are not making space for the next blessing to show up in your life. Let go of grudges, anger, and jealousy. Let go of racial biases and prejudices. Let go of guilt and shame.

Practice letting go of strong emotions, such as jealousy and anger. Learn to experience it, breathe through it, feel it and then be free. Let it go. It will become easier to let go, over and over again, over time and with practice.

Don't Take It Personal

Aparigraha is learning to not take it personal. Whatever people do or say, don't take it personal. Let go of the need to be praised by other people or the need for ally cookies[16]. So, if someone calls you out for racist language or behavior, don't take it personally. It is not about changing who you are, but it is about transforming racist thoughts and beliefs.

---

[16] Ally cookies is when someone helps an oppressed person or group of oppressed people because they want "credit" or "cookies." It is a term used to gently mock such attention seeking.

"White fragility"[17] is a phrase coined by author Dr. Robin DiAngelo. She explains how certain patterns make it difficult for many white people to understand racism as a system and that leads to the dynamics of white fragility. Even a minimum amount of racial stress becomes intolerable, triggering a range of defensive actions.

We have to let go of the notion that bad people are racist and good people are not. Racism is systemic; if you are unaware or asleep to this truth, then you may be unknowingly perpetuating or complicit in white supremacy in various ways. Don't take it personally; allow it to open your eyes.

Layla Saad explains, "White fragility shows up as white people getting angry, defensive, afraid, arguing, claiming they're being shamed, crying or simply falling silent and choosing to check out of the conversation."

If someone calls out your racist language or behavior, don't take it personally. Instead, pause, listen carefully, receive, reflect and change your behavior. If you take it personally and your white fragility shows up, it will prevent you from having a meaningful conversation about race. If you take it personally, you will go into fight-or-flight mode, causing you to stay silent, avoid the difficult conversation, or become combative.

One of the goals in yoga is overcoming the ego. Freud referred to the ego as the "conscious mind or the awareness that we are a being with an identity." The ego is not problematic, it is the over attachment to the ego that presents a problem. When you attach to your story, your thoughts, your body and mind, then you lose your true self, your

---

[17] White fragility is when a white person becomes uncomfortable or defensive when confronted with racial inequality and injustice. The term "white fragility" was coined by Dr. Robin DiAngelo in a 2011 journal article.

essence. If your "white fragility" shows up during a conversation about race, it means your ego has shown up. Slow down, pause, watch your breath and watch your thoughts. Become a witness to your true self.

Don Miguel Ruiz writes from The Four Agreements, "Don't take anything personally."

Whatever people do or say, don't take it personally. Even if they tell you how awesome you are, don't take it personally. You know you are awesome. Let go of the need to be praised by other people. If you obsess over what other people think of you, whether it be good or bad, you will always be their prisoner. Let your inner voice, your awakened self, speak louder than the opinions of others, in order to live authentically.

What happens when someone says something critical or mean to you? Do you allow their words to upset you? Do you take it personally? You may not only fear judgment from other people, but often suffer from your own self-judgment or inner critic. Your inner critic is robbing you of your innate goodness, worth, talent and ability. The inner critic makes you believe in illusions, and it causes chaos in your mind. Begin to notice what happens when negative thoughts arise. Do you believe them? Do you feel small? Your inner critic may not go away completely, but you can pause and become aware of your critical thoughts. Replace your critical thoughts with more accurate and positive statements. In that moment, you are able to regain your power and develop a new positive habit.

Let Go and Trust the Process

Aprarigraha or nonpossessiveness reminds you to let go and trust the process. Uncovering the truth and changing your behavior takes time; it's a process. Instead of grasping and clinging, let go, stay open and find ways to nurture, educate and center yourself so you feel strong, confident and independent.

Anti-racism work is a lifelong practice. You will not "get it right" on day one. You will make mistakes, and that is how you learn and grow. Anti-racism work requires you to be vulnerable and courageous. Expand your comfort zone gradually, remember to breathe, apologize when needed, and take responsibility. As you gain confidence in this practice, you will find more ease in surrendering to the truth. Begin today and commit for a lifetime.

Aparigraha, nonpossessiveness, reminds you to let go of attachments, the need for praise, and white fragility, and instead to focus on living and loving without the need to possess or take things personally. Appreciate each and every moment, fully and completely, just as it is. Do you want to be free, truly free? Learn to let go, again and again.

Setting Your Intention Meditation: Setting and Letting Go

Sit or lie down in a comfortable position
Close your eyes or soften your gaze
Take a deep breath in,
and exhale a cleansing breath through your mouth
Continue breathing through your nose, full and complete breaths

As you exhale, let go and release anything that is not serving you
Release any thoughts, ideas, beliefs, feelings,
not serving your highest purpose
Let it go
More and more, let go
Aim to let go of any shame, guilt, fear or defensiveness

As you inhale, begin to connect to the spaciousness
of your inner body
It is not empty space but open space you have created,
full of potential
Continue to breathe into that open space for a few more
rounds of breath
Deepen your connection to your breath, to your body,
and to unlimited possibility
With each breath, open your mind and open your heart
Now, as you inhale, invite a new intention, a new thought
or belief for something you would like to manifest
in the coming days, weeks, or months

Set your personal intention now or choose something clear
and open like, "I am inhaling living to my fullest potential"
Exhale and surrender to the moment, to the now
As you inhale, set your intention for the world you believe in,
the world you would you like to create
Silently say,
I Am
I Can
I Will
I Do

Breathe
Take a few more full breaths into your intention
Imagine planting it like a seed in your soul
Planting seeds of change
Planting a path to peace
Ask the Universe to support and guide you
Be clear about what you want
Take action
Then, let go
Trust the Universe
Trust the process
It will be, when the time is right
Take a few more slow,
full and complete breaths before opening your eyes
Return to gentle easy breaths through your nose
Take your time
When you are ready, slowly open your eyes
Namaste, and so it is

Aparigraha ~ Nonpossessiveness Reflection Questions

1. What things have people said that you have taken personally? Can you recall a time when someone called out your racist or biased language or behavior? How has that shaped how you live your life?

2. What beliefs, things, people, emotions (fear, anger, jealousy, sadness, guilt, grief, resentment) are you ready to let go of?

3. Explore what is standing in your way to doing this work. Is there anything you haven't let go of so you can step into who you are fully and completely? It's time to set yourself free!

6 Yama Review

The Yamas

The Yamas, or restraints, are guidelines that teach you how to live in peace and harmony with the world. Following these guidelines allows you to see beyond your own desires into the collective good. Practicing the Yamas offers a core of mindful anti-racism and self-reflection practices, and provides healing and liberation.

Yama Review

AHIMSA: NONVIOLENCE
Asks you to open your heart and mind, to do no harm, to recognize your power and privilege, and to respect the relationship you have with yourself, others and the planet.

SATYA: TRUTHFULNESS
Encourages you to become your true authentic self and asks you to look at the truth of who you are, the truth of your impact on those around you, and the truth of the world.

ASTEYA: NONSTEALING
Reminds you to focus on your abundance and how you would like to authentically impact the world. It reminds you to acknowledge your power, privilege and impact. Appreciate, don't appropriate as you identify and cultivate your skills and abilities. Save your toxic criticism, and deepen your love.

BRAHMACHARYA: NONEXCESS
Reminds you to let go of distractions and excess, and instead to rest and recharge. Focus your energy and efforts to align with fairness, equality, justice and the Divine.

APARIGRAHA: NONPOSSESSIVENESS
Reminds you to let go of attachments and white fragility, instead focus on living and loving without the need to possess or take things personally. Appreciate each and every moment, fully and completely, just as it is. Do you want to be free, truly free? Learn to let go, again and again.

7 Saucha ~ Purity

The first Niyama or yoga guideline is Saucha, a Sanskrit word that means purity. It means removing what is toxic in your life: thoughts, words and actions, people, places, and things. Saucha means cleanliness and clarity. It's about cleansing your inner being and peeling back layers to reveal your true essence.

Saucha is an inward journey of clarity. It helps you remember who you are at your core. It reminds you to connect with your outer and inner purity. Saucha requires you to let go of your baggage so you can see clearly and arrive fully. It asks you to not only seek purity with yourself, but to also be purely in the moment, just as it is. Let go of distorting or fixing, and just arrive completely, as is.

Treat your body like a temple. Fill your temple with positivity, good health and well-being.

Detox from the Inside Out

"Yoga is 90% undoing." ~Unknown

Much of awakening involves undoing: undoing bad habits, undoing old habits, undoing negative thinking, undoing harmful patterns, undoing the need to always be achieving and simply becoming more and more your True Self. You don't have to get anywhere; you just have to realize you are the divine living inside.

The practice of yoga places a priority on purifying processes such as, neti or nasal cleansing, pranayama (breathing practices), asanas (postures), meditation and following the guidelines, the Yamas and Niyamas. Purifying will look different for each person at different times in their life.

Remove Toxic People from Your Life

On the journey to freedom and purity, there is a lot of letting go and removing negativity. If often means letting go of a way of thinking that is harmful or letting go of people that cause you pain. Following this guideline empowers you to do difficult things that are also the right thing. It could mean breaking up with someone you care about, loving a relative from a distance, letting go of an old or new friend, standing up and speaking out about injustices. The important thing is to know that you have the power and the right to create a safe and positive space for yourself and others.

If it is hard to breathe and simply be your true self around someone, then they probably need to go. It doesn't matter if someone is a family member, lover, co-worker, friend, or new acquaintance. You don't have to make space for people who cause you pain, spread negativity and lies, disrespect you, disappoint you, criticize you, offend you or make you feel small. If someone accepts responsibility for their behavior and makes an effort to change, then that is a relationship worth your time.

But if someone disregards your feelings, ignores your boundaries and continues to treat you badly, they need to go.

Take note: not all toxic people are cruel and uncaring. Some are family and love you dearly, but if they tear you down rather than lift you up, you must let them go. Confronting or distancing yourself from harmful people does not mean you hate them; it means you actively love and respect yourself. Love yourself enough to say no to others and set boundaries.

Tips for removing toxic people from your life:

1. Don't expect them to change.
If you let go of the desire to change them, truly accept them for who they are, it's easier to let them go.

2.Establish and maintain boundaries.
Create a boundary checklist for what you will tolerate from partners, family members, colleagues and friends, then firmly enforce these boundaries.

3. Don't be pulled into crises.
Toxic people create dramas deliberately in order to attract more attention and engage in manipulation. Don't feel bad; break the cycle of running to their side.

Practicing saucha means not staying silent when it comes to issues of race. Let people know that toxic language, racist "jokes" or comments are not okay. Learn and practice the skills of challenging oppressive remarks, behaviors, policies, and institutional structures. If you are working for or with someone who has been called out for racism or causing harm, you will need to decide if you can continue to actively support that person or company and at the same time support and protect Black or marginalized people. Are you complicit in some way by continuing the partnership?

Advice for speaking up to your family and friends.

Speaking out against injustices takes courage and can be difficult at first. You will feel better when you learn to speak up instead of remaining silent when it comes up. And believe me, it will! Each time you speak up, you will gain more confidence and the skills to have these difficult conversations and to spread awareness.

Try the following to help people examine their thoughts/words:

1. "I need to stop you there because something you just said is not accurate. Why did you say…?"

2. "I'm having a reaction to that comment. Let's go back for a minute. Can you clarify?"

3. "Do you think you would say that if someone from that identity group was with us in the room?"

The following are things to consider before calling out someone or an institution on racist or harmful behavior/practices:

How do they typically handle instances of racial discrimination? What is the ask? Do you want them to apologize? Get fired? Stop the action? Stop partnering with a brand? Review and reform their policies? Minimize racial bias in hiring? Hire a Black advisory board? Recruit more diversity in management? Cultural sensitivity training?[18]

Purify Body, Thoughts, Words and Actions

Practice yoga, meditation and mindfulness to cleanse your mind of negative thoughts and your body of negative emotions. Learn to be fluid with your expression of emotions. Do not fear, hide, or deny them, but learn to express them in a healthy and sustainable way. People often try to avoid their feelings, but you need your feelings to find meaning in your life and to grow stronger. Feeling your emotions makes you stronger. Your feelings are energy and they shape who you are. Nothing would matter without your feelings.

Purifying and releasing toxicity means taking care of your body through proper nutrition, plenty of sleep and exercise. It means surrounding yourself with people who vibrate on a high frequency. It also means finding a way to heal traumatic experiences that you have endured as a child or presently. Healing oppressive or traumatic experiences you went through is a profound way to release toxicity. However seemingly small, these experiences have shaped you. Releasing toxicity means developing the ability to forgive (not necessarily forget) others, and most importantly, to forgive yourself. Forgiveness does not change the past, but it does change the future. Let go and trust the process.

---

[18] Adapted from Ericka Hart.

Discover and Embrace Who You Are

Internalized oppression is when members of oppressed or marginalized groups hold an oppressive view toward their own group, or they start to affirm negative stereotypes of themselves. The person may feel a sense of inferiority.

As people of color are victimized by racism, we internalize it. We may develop beliefs, actions, and behaviors that support or collude with racism. Internalized racism has its own reality and consequences in communities of color. There is a system in place that expands the power and privilege of white people and that actively undermines the power of BIPOC and their communities.

Internalized racism is not the same as self-hatred and low self-esteem because it is structural. Even people of color with high self-esteem will have to untangle the internalized racism that infects our black and brown lives and communities.

Anti-Blackness

You may have seen the videos that surfaced of a young Black man that was forced to cut off his dreadlocks during a wrestling match. The prominent question was why did so many people watch and allow this to happen? Anti-Blackness lies invisibly in the back of the mind. Most people are taught not to see it, not in your actions or inactions, words or silence. Anti-Blackness affects your behavior and has a huge impact on your life and the life of others. It prevents you from seeing other people's humanity. It may lead you to believe that Black people deserve what happens to them. Black Americans are typically assumed to be at fault or blamed for being mistreated. According to FBI statistics, between 2005 and 2012 in the United States, white police officers killed an average of two Black Americans per week. What will it take for more white people to show concern, express outrage and take action?

White people are socialized to identify as white and internalize the messages that white is the norm and superior race. Reflecting on your anti-Blackness is an intense process of examining and unlearning. Anti-Blackness isn't limited to white people. Non-Black people of color can perpetuate anti-Blackness too. Everyone has to look at how they may be perpetuating anti-Blackness in their everyday life.

"Be yourself; everyone else is already taken." ~Oscar Wilde

In high school, I wore my hair natural for one week. One day, as I was walking home from school, a few girls started singing, "Who's that girl with the nappy hair?" Then they started cracking up, laughing. I was mortified. As a mixed race Black woman, hair has always been a self-discovery and self-loving journey for me. I grew up internalizing messages that said I shouldn't accept my natural hair, skin tone, or my natural features. I used to use toxic chemicals to straighten my hair because I wasn't comfortable with my natural hair. I thought it was too curly, too kinky, too nappy, too ugly. I had big beautiful curly hair long before the "big hair, don't care" naturally curly movement.[19]

When I was about 26 years old, I did my first "big chop." I cut off all my hair and started wearing my hair natural; I felt free. I felt myself letting go of negative thoughts about my hair, my culture and about

---

[19] California Gov. Gavin Newsom signed the CROWN act into law alongside State Sen. Holly Mitchell, making California the first state to officially ban racial discrimination against people wearing certain natural hairstyles.

myself. I was letting go of all the parts of me that were rejecting my Blackness, my true, pure self.

After I had been wearing my hair natural for a few years, I went to a yoga teacher gathering. I was the only Black yoga teacher at this gathering, and I didn't know anyone. I was feeling a little awkward and out of place. This woman walked up to me, stared at my hair, tried to touch it and said, "Sonia, YOUR hair—it looks so alive." I really did not know what to say in response. Her astonishment and microaggression left me speechless.

Please do not touch Black women's or children's hair. If you were fascinated by someone's buttocks, you would not reach out and touch them. Avoid giving unsolicited comments or inauthentic compliments to Black women about their hair. While our hair is not who we are, it is a part of our body and our being. Our hair holds many stories, it is sacred.

It takes time to reject the lies that have been fed to you. The hair journey is not the same experience for all Black women. Many straighten their hair, and it doesn't mean they are less accepting of their true self. For me, self-acceptance, self-love and undoing internalized racism was a process of accepting my naturally curly, kinky hair, and recognizing the beauty and uniqueness of it.

I want my children and all children to grow up knowing their natural hair is beautiful. And most importantly, to love all parts of themselves. My 7-year-old daughter has already experienced one of her peers at school telling her that her dreadlocks look weird. My 10-year-old son was disappointed and hurt when one of his friends at school told him that his Golden State Warriors NBA basketball jersey that said "The Town" on it, should say "The Hood" because he is Black.

I don't want my kids to grow up with a sense of shame for the things that make them different, or shame for the culture from which they come from. This is often what it means to grow up as a person of color in a white-dominated world. This is the world I grew up in. This is not the world I want to leave behind. I want to live in a world where children of color don't spend their entire childhood wishing to be in a different skin.

Currently, my dreadlock journey is representative of my spiritual journey. My locs mean fully embracing myself, and they express freedom, strength, and reverence for my ancestors. My locs have taught me patience, humility and love. They are a protest to Eurocentric beauty standards and the anti-Blackness inherent in those standards that are promoted around the world and embedded into our daily lives. I want people to see me and know that I am not ashamed of my Blackness but fully embrace it.

Saucha Journey

"It's systematic of people, Black people included, not being
divorced from whiteness. We have to constantly give it up."
~Ebony Donnelly

The saucha journey is to discover who you are and what you are meant to express. It's about undoing, unlearning and untangling. Become aware of distorting yourself, attaching to whiteness, internalizing Eurocentric beauty standards, or internalizing racism, and instead, focus on illuminating the parts of yourself that are unseen. Illuminate and celebrate the parts of yourself that make you different and unique. I will never forget on the second date with my husband when he said to me, "You have more to offer than you show." In that moment, I felt seen.

What will it take for you to love yourself fiercely just as you are? Your true power is when you accept yourself for who you are; then, you allow space to accept others for exactly who they are. Make space for yourself and others to be exactly who they are in this world.

Saucha, purity, is a reminder of pure and compassionate thoughts, speech and actions. It is about removing toxins from your heart, body, mind, soul and surroundings, to reveal your shine, your True Self. Saucha journey is about discovering, examining and embracing who you are, your core essence.

Spiritual Detox Meditation: Removing Toxins From Your Mind

Sit or lie down in a comfortable position
Close your eyes or soften your gaze
Take a deep breath in
and exhale a cleansing breath through your mouth

Continue breathing through your nose, full and complete breaths

Sense your breath and sense your body
Scan your body with attention from the crown of your head
down to your toes
Soften your shoulders and your neck
Soften your jaw and around your mouth
Soften around the eyes and your brow

Continue to direct your attention to the sensations in your body
As thoughts arise,
continue to anchor your attention into the present moment

Notice when your thoughts are interpreting, judging,
measuring, or expecting
This process consumes vital energy and builds anxiety
Continue to redirect your attention to your body and breath
Reclaim the energy

Allow your attention to your breath to bring you into the

present moment

Stay present
Pure body
Pure and open mind
Pure and open heart
Clear mind, open heart

Sense the vibrancy of your body, your being
Sense pure light
Sense freedom

Take a few more slow,
full and complete breaths before opening your eyes

Return to gentle easy breaths through your nose

When you are ready, slowly open your eyes

Namaste, and so it is

Saucha ~ Purity Reflection Questions

1. Who do you need to forgive or let go of in order to release toxins from your life?

2. Can you practice breaking the silence and speaking up when you hear or see racism, bias or toxic behavior?

3. Can you identify how you may have internalized anti-Blackness? If so, what steps can you take towards undoing and unlearning those beliefs?

4. Is there anything about yourself that you have difficulty loving fiercely? If so, what steps can you take towards loving that part of yourself? If you are a person of color, can you identify how you may have internalized racism? If so, what steps can you take to actualizing your full humanity, power and wisdom?

8 Santosha ~ Contentment

"Abundance is not something we acquire; it is something we tune into." ~Wayne Dyer

The second Niyama or yoga guideline is Santosha, a Sanskrit word that means contentment. You can't achieve contentment without a deep sense of gratitude. Focus your energy on positivity, gratitude, and abundance and you will bring more of these things into your life. Santosha is feeling ease and at peace with yourself and your lifestyle. Santosha means accepting and appreciating all that you have and all that you are right now.

Practice gratitude daily for what you do have. You cannot wait to live the life you want. You need to live it, right now, today. You may not have everything that you want, but you live with a heart full of gratitude for everything that you do have. Instead of obsessing over what you want or desire, or on all the things that you think will make you happy, direct your focus on all the things you have that bring you joy and gratitude.

Vibrate Higher

Keep your vibration high by doing things you love. Do more of what makes you happy. When you are happy, you are magnetic. When you are happy and enjoying your life, you draw more goodness to you. Keep your vibration high and you will draw what you want to you more quickly. Be aware, you will draw the good, the bad and the in-between. You will need to make good decisions about what you allow to flow into your life and stay there.

Start doing what you love, NOW. Don't wait until you have more time or more money. Do what you can today. Move toward what you want to create daily and be sure that your actions, words, and thoughts support what you want. Your self-talk statements, your community, your beliefs, and everything you surround yourself with need to be things aligned with maintaining a high vibration.

State what you want to do in the present. If you want to be a writer, then say, "I am a writer," instead of saying, "I want to be a writer." Envision what you want, but more importantly, act as though it's already happening. Be that writer. Write!

Gratitude Cultivates a Kind and Loving Heart

Gratitude makes you more open-hearted, giving, and generous, not for rewards, for "unattached giving." Can you open your heart and see all beings with love? Can you open your heart and see yourself with love? Say this prayer of two simple words, "Thank you." Practice gratitude daily and you will improve your emotional health and well-being. Practice gratitude to stay rooted in it. The moment is what it is. It is complete. Accept and surrender to what is.

Gratitude Makes You Less Self/ White Centered

Gratitude increases spiritualism and makes you less self-centered. The more spiritual you are, the more likely you are to be grateful. A compassion and gratitude practice can help you to see the needs of others. This doesn't mean that you stop putting yourself first, but you learn to live in a more inclusive and equal way with all people.

How do you react when you are not centered in spaces and conversations? Ask yourself if you expect your partner, your job, or your children to meet all your needs. If so, you may find yourself frustrated and disappointed when things are not going your way. Instead, ask yourself, what is it that I am here to learn? Pause, take a deep breath and surrender to what is. This will build your ability to be patient and rooted during challenging times, and it will create a deep sense of calm around you. You have the power over your emotional state and the ability to live fully in contentment.

White-Centered

We live in a culture where white is "normal" and others are marginalized. White being normal makes everything else abnormal. The world nearly revolves around white people. Learn from and listen closely to people who are not white, be grateful for their perspective, and act with their best interests in mind.

When I was in middle school, a girl said, "Sonia is pretty for a Black girl." This is a horribly offensive microaggression. It affirms a belief that there is something unattractive and fundamentally wrong with being a person of color. White women can be regarded as pretty simply for being white. We are socialized to believe that white is pretty and black is not, and by doing so, we are perpetuating racism.

African American culture is one of the most under-appreciated, under-valued, and under-resourced assets in America. African American culture or Black culture in the United States is a unique and dynamic culture that has had and continues to have a profound impact on America and the world. Nonetheless, no white person grows up not knowing it is more beneficial to be white. White people benefit from institutional racism, inequality, and profoundly unequal schools. There is extreme individualism, focused on getting your child the best of everything, rather than focused on all children receiving the best education possible. I've witnessed parents unsure of sending their children to the middle school in our neighborhood because of the children from the other schools that will be attending. Those children from other schools are children of color and/or children who come from families with less income. Sadly, the absence of people of color determines the value of our schools and neighborhoods. It's a "good" school because it is predominantly white. It is a "good" neighborhood because it is predominantly white. She is a "good" person or pretty because she is white.

As a white person, what can I do to undo white being "normal" and others being marginalized? How do we begin to live reparatively?

Begin by acknowledging that being white does come with privilege and advantages. Notice if you are making conversations about race all about you and your feelings. It is true that you may have experienced bias or anti-whiteness in your life. However, remember that racism is systemic. It is not only about individual acts, but about the systems and structures in place that uphold inequality and injustices. Acknowledge the pain and suffering that Black people have and continue to endure. Break your silence around racism and begin to work with other white people and challenge white people and white centering. Talk about dismantling racism in white spaces that people of color do not have access to. Learn by being in relationship with other races. Aim to do less harm and be accountable. Know that you will make mistakes; that is inevitable, and it is how you learn. Disrupting racism requires you to change the way you live. The commitment needs to be much stronger, especially from yogis, liberals and progressives. Taking action, whether big or small, is necessary to create change.

Embrace Your Life

Contentment is not the fulfillment of what you want, but the realization of how much you already have. Everything has purpose in your life. Be content and at ease with what you have. Avoid thinking, if only I could get that big raise, a new car, a new house or have children, then I would finally be happy. Looking outward will always end up disappointing you. There is true freedom and contentment in taking life as it comes to you, the love and the loss, the confusion and the clarity, the pleasure and the pain. This doesn't mean you do not aspire for more, but you start from a place of gratitude for what you do have, and surrender to what is right now. Welcome the moment. Be in the moment. Be content with where you are and what you have right here, right now.

Can contentment and ambition coexist?

Contentment brings peace and gratitude, but that doesn't mean you aren't actively searching for your calling or purpose in life or actively working for justice and equality. When you are content, you may not have the best of everything but you MAKE the best of everything. A content person with a grateful heart still wants to DO better and BE better. Passion is important; pursue everything with (com)passion. Find you passion and you will find your purpose.

Fiercely Love Your Life.

This is the gift: you are alive. Every day. Every moment. Alive. You can live for tomorrow, or you can live for today. You can live your best life, right now, in this moment. Discover your truth and continue becoming that person. Open your eyes and heart to the wonder of this moment. You are complete right now. Life is complete right now.

Santosha, contentment, reminds you to focus on abundance and gratitude to become less self-centered and less white-centered. Cultivate a deep sense of gratitude, and love others, yourself and your life, just as it is.

Gratitude Meditation: Thank You

Sit or lie down in a comfortable position
Close your eyes or soften your gaze

Inhale, "Thank"
Exhale, "you"
Relax your body and feel gratitude at your heart center

Surrender to your heart and not your head
Give gratitude the opportunity to come up naturally
Allow yourself to sink into the feeling

Bring your awareness to your breath
Inhale, draw love in
Exhale, release love out

As you inhale, feel your heart expand
As you exhale, feel your heart soften

Bring your awareness to your abundance
Your expansion
Your evolution
Your flow and rhythm with life
The potential of every moment

Breathe and feel ease
Feel love at your heart center

Shift your attention to the loved ones in your life
Sense the love you have for your loved ones
Sense the love you have for yourself
Your body
Your breath
Your everything

Open your heart and see all beings with love
Open your heart and see yourself with love

Be content with each moment, just as it is
There is nothing missing
The moment is complete, as it is
Pause and receive

Allow yourself to be in each moment
Fully and completely
Just as it is, surrender
Inhale, "Thank,"
Exhale, "you"

Just breathe, easy gentle breaths through your nose

Take your time
When you are ready, open your eyes
Namaste, and so it is

Santosha ~ Contentment Reflection Questions

1. I am grateful for... list at least five things. List things you can do to keep your vibration high daily.

2. What, if anything, are you seeking outside of yourself for fulfillment and contentment? How can you shift this?

3. Are you identifying white as being the "norm"? How has this shaped your life?

4. Replace negative thoughts and biases with love and gratitude. Identify and write down the negative thoughts or biases that sometimes surface. What words or mantras can you replace them with?

9 Tapas ~ Self-Discipline

"You gain strength, courage and confidence by every experience in which you really stop to look fear in the face."
~Eleanor Roosevelt

Discipline : Determined : Inner Fire

The third Niyama or yoga guideline is Tapas, a Sanskrit word that means self-discipline. Tapas is having an inner fire that propels you to reach your fullest potential. The inner fire sparks the divinity in you. Tapas is courage, passion, and fiery discipline used to burn away impurities and pave the way to your true greatness.

Direct your focus to engage life and achieve the ultimate goal of creating union with the Divine or alignment with the Source. Tapas helps to burn away all desires that stand in your way of this goal.

It is in your darkest times of pain, loss and confusion that your character and undeniable strength are born. You have no idea what your full potential is, but through the dark times, your True Self is slowly revealed to you. The best is buried in the depths of you. Your future is bright and shiny if you are willing to put forth the effort to live your best life right now.

Challenge Yourself to Be Uncomfortable

Challenge yourself to be uncomfortable; that is where growth happens. Be willing to go through and expand in difficult times. After the storm, after the rain, there are clear skies. Your failures are your lessons. Your lessons are your blessings. There is just as much equity in failing as there is in succeeding. Learn to fail and then try again. Chaka Khan sings, "Through the fire, to the limit, to the wall." On the other side of difficult times is a stronger, wiser you.

I love the saying, "It's not about who you are when everything is going your way; it's about who you are when nothing is going your way."

Going to college was not something my parents encouraged or prepared me to do. My sister and I are the first in our family to earn a college degree. I had never been on a college campus prior to attending UC Berkeley. My parents did not take me on any college tours, and I knew very little about it, but earning a college degree was always a strong desire that I had within me. Fortunately, in high school I met an amazing Black female teacher who was instrumental in helping me get into Cal Berkeley.

Most of what I knew about college came from the television show, A Different World, with Lisa Bonet, Kadeem Hardison, Jada Pinkett Smith and Jasmine Guy. I didn't attend a HBCU (historically Black colleges and universities), so in order to be around Black students, I chose to move into the African American Theme House at UC Berkeley. It wasn't exactly like the tv show, but I did meet two of my best friends in the Afro House.

When I finally reached the university, what I had dreamt of and worked for, it was like learning a new language. I felt alienated and out of place. My ideas and writing were never about theory, but about personal feelings and how it relates to life. I remember sitting in my ethnic studies classroom of 30 students, and the graduate instructor asked, "What is worse: overt racism or covert racism?" I was in shock at the absurdity of the question, and could not speak, but a young white woman immediately spoke up. She said, "Covert [racism] is better. I know someone whose grandmother cannot stand Black people, but she would never say it to their face." It seems that California is full of covert racists even in the most liberal cities. Since racism is systemic, being a covert racist is not better than being an overt racist. It's actually much more difficult to disrupt covert racism, since it is disguised and subtle. Covert racism is fertile ground for gaslighting[20] to occur.

I experienced difficult times while I was at UC Berkeley. I struggled financially throughout my undergraduate years. My parents divorced when I was eighteen years old and had their own financial struggles, so I ended up with a $30,000[21] student loan debt and a Bachelor of Arts Degree in Social Welfare. I was definitely challenged, burnt and blessed by that degree.

---

[20] Gaslighting is a form of psychological manipulation that seeks to sow seeds of doubt in a targeted individual or in members of a targeted group, making them question their own memory, perception, and sanity.

[21] According to the U.S. Department of Education, seventy-two percent of Black students go into debt to pay for their educations.

The Fiery Discipline of Practice

"Practice, and all is coming." ~Pattabhi Jois

When you practice, you use your skills and you build upon them. You begin to explore pushing past old edges and play with discovering new ones. You improve with practice. People often overlook the power and importance of practice. Practice refines your body and mind to perform a task beautifully, effortlessly, strongly and gracefully. The way a yogi practices vinyasa krama, carefully synchronizing their breath and body in asanas, or the way NBA basketball player Stephen Curry shoots 3-pointers. Your body is magic. A miracle. The greatest, most spiritual experiences happen in the body, not in the head. Movement connects you to the moment, like when Stephen Curry is in the zone, making not one impossible shot, but many. Practice for the pure joy and love of it. Practice, prepare, and get into a zone.

As a child, I competed in artistic roller skating. I practiced 5 to 7 days a week, had two lessons per week, and there was a time when I got up at 5am to practice before school. At one point, I was training for a regional championship that took place in Bakersfield, California. Our freestyle routines were 2 minutes and 45 seconds long, filled with a variety of jumps and spins. It may not sound very long, but it was. I would be completely out of breath and exhausted by the end. To prepare for the competition, my skating coach made me perform three routines consecutively at the end of my lesson. While I performed the routine, he followed me around on the skating floor, yelling instructions and verbally pushing me to keep going. Normally, the coach would just sit in the sound booth and watch the routine, but he was following me to make sure I didn't give up.

By the time I got to the second routine, I didn't have any energy to over-think things; I just had to perform, jump, spin, and skate my heart out. Be in the moment. It was brutal and intense, but it actually worked. I performed one of my best routines at the regional competition and advanced to the finals. I did not end up placing, but I was out there competing with the top 10 girls in the region, after suffering from an earlier injury.

In yoga, a daily disciplined practice is called sadhana. It is a tool used to work on yourself physically, mentally, and spiritually. It is a daily practice to achieve the ultimate goal of union with the Divine or alignment with the Source. Be unattached to the end goal and dive into the wonder of your practice. Fall in love with your practice. Motivation and inspiration will come and go, but your practice will always be there for you. Practice is instrumental in continuing your growth and improvement.

The brain has the ability to build habits, beliefs, and emotional responses to one thing. The beautiful thing is you can shape your brain with practice and with the repetition of yoga, meditation, affirmations, and reflections. You can shape your brain to think in a more life-affirming way and release old ways of thinking and being that no longer serve you. It will take tapas, discipline, determination and a commitment to a consistent practice.

"I learned that courage was not the absence of fear, but the triumph over it. The brave man is not he who does not feel afraid, but he who conquers that fear." ~Nelson Mandela

Courageous Conversations About Race

Courageous conversations about race can be uncomfortable, challenging, and painful. Trust me, I am often uncomfortable too. Talking about racism is very painful and emotional, but necessary to create change. Living as a person of color in a racist society is even more painful. In order to bridge the divide of race, meaningful conversations grounded in shared understanding is needed. People of color and white people are ready to engage in conversation, in protest, and in forward movement.

Before having conversations about race, recognize your bias and privilege. Identify whatever race-based bias you hold and confront it. Part of the privilege associated with whiteness is the luxury of not having to consider one's own race or acknowledge the disadvantages faced by many people of color. As you begin to have conversations about racism or other forms of oppression, avoid tone policing.[22] Learn to become comfortable with your truth, realize where you are in the process, and take action to dismantle racism.

It will take practice to become better equipped to talk about racism and to cultivate positive change. Don't worry about being wrong; worry about not uncovering the truth.

"The beauty of anti-racism is that you don't have to pretend to be free of racism to be anti-racist. Anti-racism is the commitment to fight racism wherever you find it, including in yourself. And it's the only way forward." ~Ijeoma Oluo

---

[22] Tone policing is criticizing a person for expressing emotion when talking about oppression. It focuses on the person's tone rather the message itself.

Practice talking about race.

Start with yourself. Reflect on your own identity, race, and privileges. Read about Black lives and whiteness. You can't talk about racism without talking about whiteness. Then, go deeper. Begin talking with friends, family, co-workers, and teachers. If you are a parent, talk to your children about race and racism.

Facing Your Fears

Get to the root of your fears. You did not come to earth to live a fear-based life. Allow yourself to go deeper within until you realize that fear is rooted in limited beliefs and it limits your own experience of life.

How can I overcome the fear of taking about race?

It is normal to have a lot of fear or discomfort while talking about race because (white) people have avoided the conversation for years. You can learn to talk about race without fighting or getting defensive. It will take practice. It will not be a harmonious, peaceful conversation; it will be intense, passionate and emotional. Surrender to that and trust the process.

Can you stay in the uncomfortable, in the heat, and not run away? Can you trust the process? Can you stay in order to be shaped and transformed into your greatness? Your practice prepares you to stay in the fire of life and to make the clear and compassionate choice. Are you making choices that build your strength and character and help you reach your full potential?

Tapas, self-discipline, is consciously choosing to go through the fire in order to grow and reach your full potential. It reminds you to transform your lessons into blessings, and of the importance of courage, discipline, practice, and facing your fears.

Inner Fire Meditation: Will Power

Become aware of your breathing
The rise and fall of your chest
The rise and fall of your belly
Begin to inhale fully
Exhale slowly

Inhale into your belly
Expand your abdomen as you inhale
Gently contract and firm you belly as you exhale
Cultivate a belly breath
Expanding and contracting your abdomen as your breathe

Take long slow breaths down into the navel area
Hold it there for three counts and release it
Inhale into your low belly
Pause for three counts
Slowly exhale all the way out
Repeat three times

Go deeper into the body
Into the heart
Imagine pure light radiating from your heart
Feel the warmth and the heat in your belly, at your heart center,
in every cell of your body
Sense the inner fire and let it surround you
And fill the room

Discipline is the key to freedom and independence
If you want to succeed
You need to practice self-discipline
Affirm your commitment to succeed
Push through adversity to complete your goal

In order to achieve freedom
You must face challenges and take risks and maybe lose your way
You may be tempted to give up

Connect with your inner strength and willpower
Connect with your inner sense of purpose
Breathe deeply into that sensation
Ride the wave of the breath, the ebb and flow,
the challenges and the opportunities

Focus on your inner heat and bright golden light at the heart center
Breathe into excitement and opportunity
Feel your goals as a reality
You are capable
You are committed

Resume rhythmic breathing through the nose
Clear your mind and rest, breathe easy
Take your time, when you are ready, slowly open your eyes
Namaste, and so it is

Tapas ~ Self-Discipline Reflection Questions

1. Write about a time when you were challenged around race issues and/or had a courageous conversation about race. What lessons can you identify from that event?

2. How are you fears connected to self-doubt? How is fear limiting your freedom?

3. Anything you want takes hard work, dedication and practice. Choose a daily practice or ritual to advance your goal. Write it down.

4. Listen to your inner voice and make choices that build your character. Can you describe a time when you listened to your inner voice?

10 Svadhyaya ~ Self-Study

"The soul is the truth of who we are, the light, the love, which is within us." ~Marianne Williamson

The fourth Niyama or yoga guideline is Svadhyaya, a Sanskrit word that means self-study. Svadhyaya is the process of knowing your True Self and all the layers or armor you have wrapped yourself in. It is the process of examining and reflecting on who you are. One way to dismantle racism and to cultivate an anti-racism practice is to follow the guideline svadhyaya, or self-inquiry. The path of intense self-inquiry is a difficult path.

By meditating, you are practicing your ability to witness. When you meditate, you learn to watch your thoughts and not attach. You learn to become a witness to your breath, your body sensations, and your thoughts. As you witness your outer body and the many layers you have wrapped yourself in, you use breath as a bridge to connect to your inner being, your subtle body or your soul. Once you discover and understand each layer you are wrapped in, you move closer to oneness with your True Self. The layers you are wrapped in are influenced by your race, nationality, culture, gender, ancestors, family history, education, society and personal experience. You will suffer when you identify with the layers you have wrapped yourself in and forget who you are at your core. Divine.

Live in the "I Am"

Svadhyaya is getting to the foundation of who you are and reclaiming parts of yourself you may have lost due to socialization, traumatic experiences, oppression or adopting negative or limiting beliefs about yourself. The more you understand yourself, the more you can let go of self-destructive tendencies, old habits and harmful coping mechanisms. You can begin to delete anything not serving your Higher Self.

As you heighten consciousness and awareness of each moment, every thought, every word and every action, you will see more clearly the world or reality you have created. You will see more clearly and honestly the parts of yourself you love, can't stand, or can't accept. You will also see more clearly your inner light.

Cultivate Self-Reflective Consciousness

You have to be self-aware to change anything about yourself. Increasing self-awareness through yoga and meditation may lead to the revelation of your True Self. Through self-awareness, you are able to align the rational and the emotional part of the brain. On a deep and profound level, you may understand the story or trauma of what happened to you, but you also need to connect with the emotion of it. You can know something on an intellectual level, but can you embody it on a cellular level? How does it feel when you think of these previous experiences? How are you behaving and what are the choices you are making because of these previous experiences? Is it life-affirming or destructive? How can you begin to shift your awareness and energy in a different direction? Can you begin to make better life choices? Meditation, mindfulness, and writing are some activities that cultivate self-reflective consciousness.

Shift your mindset to living in the present, the I Am, and delete the "I can't" or, "I want to be." Leave space for the unimaginable or the impossible to show up. It may not come to you in the perfect way, but it will come to you in an authentic way, revealing your authentic Self.

"To be beautiful means to be yourself. You don't need to be accepted by others. You need to accept yourself."
~Thich Nhat Hanh

I began experiencing depression around the age of 12. At 15 years old, I started drinking alcohol, a lot of it, and making bad choices. I remember thinking I just wanted to escape my reality and all of the pain I felt. In college, I would say I wanted to drink until I forgot my name. Looking back, it wasn't just that I wanted to numb myself; I wanted to erase myself.

At the age of 19, I found my first therapist on my own. I began to ask the question: Who am I? In that therapist's office, I started unpacking a lot of my pain and sorrow. I felt safe enough to share how much I desperately wanted to feel loved, connected, accepted and truly seen. Back then, I didn't know, but what I really needed was to learn to love and accept myself. I felt safe enough to cry, cry and cry and just begin to release some of my pain. Part of my sorrow came from the fact that I was not connected to who I was; I was not connected to my Blackness or grounded in my heritage. I was not raised with a strong sense of self, pride and legacy of being Black. Not my father, nor my mother, were prepared to empower and educate their mixed race Black children. I attended public elementary school, with no other Black children other than my siblings. I was conditioned to see the world through a white lens. In mainstream public school Blackness is not celebrated and African American history is limited or left out completely. I was raised with limited knowledge and consciousness of the beauty of being Black in this world. In fact, I remember one day, my granddaddy said, "I ain't no African." Slavery had made him a stranger to his homeland, Africa. He had internalized anti-African sentiments due to oppression and stereotypes perpetuated by the American culture.

It's not only white people who are conditioned to believe incorrect and negative stereotypes about Black people; Black Americans internalize these negative perceptions as well. These prejudices encourage self-criticism and often result in trying to distance ourselves from our Blackness, from who we are. I had spent much of my life running from my Blackness. But now, I was running to it, with wide open arms, and steadily becoming comfortable and confident in my skin, realizing and experiencing just how beyond beautiful Black is. The more you know about your culture and heritage, the better able you are to step into your power.

When things aren't going your way, or when you feel like you are in a dark space, it is a favorable time for growth and clarity. During these circumstances, you have the opportunity to examine more closely your identity, belief system and conditioning. You can reassess where your disappointments stem from and challenge your belief system of what is right or wrong, good or bad, superior or inferior. If you examine where you feel discomfort and what you resist learning, you will open a pathway to freedom. Change happens when each person questions their own values and beliefs, then takes the right or compassionate action.

99 Problems, but It's Never about You

It's much easier to blame others than to take responsibility for your racist actions or inaction. Don't blame an entire group of oppressed people for the current state of inequality in this country. It's important to look at the bigger picture because often times, problems are caused by corrupt systems. There is a great need to feel a sense of control over your life, and blaming others helps you maintain this false sense of control. By blaming others, you are able to avoid the unwanted feelings within yourself. When you continue to blame others, you ignore important life lessons. When you fail to learn a lesson, you will find yourself encountering that same life lesson again and again. The universe will continue to provide you with the opportunity to learn that life lesson, until you do.

> *"I have the audacity to believe that peoples everywhere can have three meals a day for their bodies, education and culture for their minds, and dignity, equality, and freedom for their spirits." ~Dr. Martin Luther King Jr.*

A white mother was telling me about how her daughter was applying to get into several different college programs. They were flying to several schools across the United States for interviews. The mother was very anxious and told me, "My daughter is very white." I really wasn't sure what she meant by it, so I replied, "The first step is knowing." She proceeded to tell me that she fears her daughter is so white that she will not stand out in the interview process. Then she said, "You know what I mean?" As I glared at her, I replied, "No, I don't."

The audacity to tell a Black mother that you are concerned about your "very white" child not being accepted into a college program because of her whiteness shows a complete disconnect and disregard for the amount of white privilege they are holding. This family has the means to apply and fly to different schools across the United States. That alone places them at an advantage. Why wasn't she focused on standing out because of her merit, talent, skill? Why was she blaming her whiteness? And why was she comfortable telling me?

Education in America is not accessible and equitable for youth of all backgrounds. Students of color are much more likely to attend high poverty schools.[23] High poverty or underperforming high schools do not have the resources to well prepare their students for higher education.

Look Closely at Your Whiteness, Your Privilege, Your Power

---

[23] According to The Atlantic, federal data shows, in almost all major American cities, most African American and Hispanic students attend public schools where a majority of their classmates qualify as poor or low-income. This is a major obstacle to creating quality education available to all American students.

DIFFERENT WAYS OF BEING WHITE
*Adapted from Unitarian Universalist Association

OVERT RACISTS
Ku Klux Klan
Hate Groups
Militia Groups
Supremacists
Segregationists
White Nationalists

MAINSTREAM RACISTS
- *These white people do see racial difference.*
- *Believe that white people are superior and people of color are inferior.*
- *Enjoy the power and privilege that white people have in this society.*
- *Blame people of color for their problems.*
- *They are not interested in working for racial justice but will do things to keep the peace.*

LIBERAL RACISTS
- *Assume the white way of life is the norm.*
- *Value multi-cultural diversity but on their own terms. "I will accept you if you think and behave like me."*
- *For some, image is important. Often want to look good. "See I am not prejudiced. I am trying to help."*
- *Understand the oppression of people of color, but act by trying to help, fix, or save people of color.*
- *Don't address the realities of white power and privilgege.*

ANTI-RACIST
- *Do not see whiteness as the norm.*
- *Value racial and cultural diversity.*
- *Willing to challenge white power and privilege.*
- *Strive to be allies with anti-racist leaders from people of color communities.*
- *Develop accountability structures with people of color leaders for their anti-racism work.*

No matter how awake you think you are, you likely have unexamined privilege. Your unexamined privilege is influencing your thoughts, words, and actions in a way that may be harmful to others. Examining your privilege provides an opportunity to make change at the intersection of your advantage and someone else's disadvantage. As a light skinned, cisgendered, able bodied person, I am benefiting from those privileges. I have to challenge that because if I don't speak up, then I may be perpetuating it. The actress, Amandla Stenberg, turned down a Black Panther role due to her light skinned privilege. Challenging privilege will sometimes mean giving up your advantages to make space for those who are often treated unequally.

You must not be afraid to look at the truth of yourself and the world. Look at the disharmony, the pain within, the injustices, inequality, oppression, police brutality, suffering and horror in the world. Don't be afraid to speak up and stand up for what's right. Are you willing to understand your whiteness or privilege? Can you get to a place where you don't need to defend, deflect or resist the truth? How can you have compassion for the parts of yourself that you are not proud of and slowly peel back those layers? How do you see the selfishness, greed and anger in the world and in yourself but cultivate your divinity?

Liberation From Suffering

Liberation is when you can release the (white) guilt and accept responsibility. Getting stuck or wallowing in white guilt centers you and makes racism all about you. Instead, allow white guilt to motivate you to take action, helping you to focus on changing your beliefs, ending racism and committing to an anti-racism practice. Emotional pain and deep reflection need to lead to action.

The intergenerational trauma of racism and the everyday occurrences of racial microaggressions take a toll on the minds and bodies of people of color. The feelings that result from being oppressed can be both paralyzing and maddening. As a defense or coping mechanism, many people will often escape or leave their body, but liberation from suffering comes from being fully present in the body. On a spiritual level, being a member of the group that benefits from oppression is no benefit at all. It becomes an obstacle to reaching your full potential and achieving liberation.

Learn to breathe through challenging yoga postures and through all the challenges in your life. Avoid hiding or denying your feelings of discomfort and pain. Learning to breathe through discomfort has the power to heal your body and mind. Breathing through discomfort is a powerful way to enhance your physical, emotional, and spiritual wellbeing. A sacred space is needed to focus inward, practicing mindful movement, becoming fully present with every sensation and every emotion; this allows the body to become a gateway to freedom and allows the integration of wholeness.

> *"Unless your consciousness is guided by principles of healing justice and revolutionary love, your spirituality cannot protect you from being an oppressor." ~Layla Saad*

Spiritual Bypassing

A spiritual journey or spiritual awakening is not about being happy all the time. It's about living in the moment, whatever that looks like. It's about being present to the truth.

Spiritual bypassing is the use of spiritual beliefs to avoid dealing with painful feelings, unresolved traumas, and conversations of racism, inequality and injustices. Heighten your awareness of spiritual bypassing in your own life and in your spiritual teachers.

> *"Spiritual bypass perpetuates the idea that the belief 'we are one' is enough to create a reality where we are treated equally. It is not enough." ~Michelle C. Johnson*

Spiritual bypassing can be focusing on the concept of "we are one" to avoid dealing with racial inequality, or it can be over-emphasizing the positive side to enlightenment, where nothing is negative. "Good vibes only." It's when you avoid talking about what needs to be discussed or looked at within your life in order to heal whatever needs to be healed.

I have witnessed quite a few yoga teachers that participate in cultural appropriation and spiritual bypassing. The following was posted on social media by a yoga teacher during the midterm elections in 2018:

"We got in just before the poll closed. It was packed with people of all ages and races...There was hope and kindness in the air... This is America. We are imperfect and we are beautiful. I am so very grateful for being able to vote and for my community of neighbors."

Widespread voter suppression, particularly against historically marginalized groups, is a reoccurring problem in the United States. During the mid-term election of 2018, severe voter suppression occurred in states with highly competitive political races and amongst people of color and low-income Americans. This is spiritual bypassing, focusing on the "kindness in the air," rather that addressing the laws that continue to keep eligible Americans from exercising the fundamental right to vote.[24]

Using the phrase, "This is America," in her post is cultural appropriation. "This Is America" is a popular song by American rapper Childish Gambino. The song addresses the issue of gun violence, the high rate of mass shootings in the United States, and the longstanding racism and discrimination against African Americans. While this spiritual white woman may not have meant to be intentionally harmful, this post's impact was incredibly harmful. She was ignoring, bypassing,

---

[24] The Voting Rights Act of 1965 prohibits racial discrimination in voting. In 2013, the Supreme Court invalidated the heart of the Voting Rights Act of 1965, freeing nine states to change their election laws.

and dismissing the truth, and in doing so, encouraging her students and followers to do the same. One of the comments from her post stated, "This is what we really are. Not what we see or (are) supposed to believe in the hyped up news."

Privilege is posting on social media without accountability. Prior to awakening, it will be challenging to see and understand one's own racist behaviors and conditioning. It takes doing the deeply spiritual work of anti-racism to begin to see more clearly.

How do you bring your suffering into beauty and turn something painful that happens into value?

The spiritual path is not always pleasurable; awakening involves growth, and growth involves pain or discomfort. People will do anything to avoid experiencing pain and facing the truth of their soul. The spiritual path is a process of making the darkness conscious. There is no coming to consciousness or awakening without moving through pain, suffering or trauma. Once you begin moving through your pain and healing your heart, then you will remember who you are at your core: Divine.

Color Blindness

"Colorblind love doesn't mean you don't talk about race. It means you talk about it more." ~Heidi W. Durrow

Examine your race-based "color blindness." The mythical color blindness movement encouraged people to not see or care about race.

It has actually served as a deflection mechanism to avoid dealing with race issues all over the world. To not see race means to deny the reality of white and black communities. It means you do not truly see me. And if you do not truly see people of color, then you cannot truly see yourself.

Get out of your comfort zone of color blindness. Learn to sit with your discomfort; allow it to be, and breathe into it. Breathe into whatever you notice. No harm will come to you if you embrace your feelings, although it may be uncomfortable. Allow yourself to feel your feelings without giving them meaning and you will notice the peace that comes from acceptance. By gently and lovingly accepting where you are, you allow space to become more compassionate with yourself and others.

For far too long we have avoided conversations about race when we should undoubtedly be talking about race. White people have been conditioned to not see their whiteness, their privilege, even as they accept the advantages of this birthright. White people can easily walk away from the conversation of race, but Black people or people of color, do not have that privilege. White people never even have to think about what it means to be white. However, I must think about what it means to be Black and how to raise my Black children in a white-dominated world every day. I must have the very important and necessary conversation with my children about how to interact with the police. It is not simply a matter of giving tips for having a positive experience with law enforcement; for Black people it may be a matter of life and death.

Even the incredibly rich and arguably greatest basketball player in the world, Lebron James, cannot avoid racism. He was a victim of a hate crime when his home was vandalized with a racial slur; "Nigger" was painted on the gate of his Brentwood estate. Oprah Winfrey, a self-made billionaire, experienced racism when a store assistant refused to show her a handbag because it was "too expensive." The Trump era has provided an opportunity to transform painful lessons into blessings. It is an opportunity for white people to heighten their awareness, hyper-examine their whiteness and take action against its inherently oppressive nature.

The practice of yoga has the potential to make a powerful impact on transformative change in the world. However, it will take more than showing up on your mat to practice asana or yoga postures. Yoga and meditation are not enough. The way yoga and meditation have been taught does not actually lead us to liberation. It's allowing people to avoid the deeper work of examining themselves in relationship to the global society. To overcome the history of inequities and create a more just society, it will take being vulnerable, having the courage to look closely at yourself and having hard conversations with people you love. It will take a willingness to sacrifice some of the advantages that come with whiteness and privilege. Yoga is a practice, and it turns out, anti-racism is a practice too.

Awakening to Your Truth

"Nobody's free until everybody's free." ~Fannie Lou Hamer

Slow down and take time to truly know yourself without judgment. Learn to watch your thoughts, words and actions in the world. The more you are able to watch or witness yourself, the more you will truly know yourself and your conditioning. Your work is to love yourself into who you are, your True Self, knowing how conditioned we all are by white supremacy.

As you begin to see your True Self, there will be a lot of letting go and undoing, peeling back layers and deep healing. Before you can heal your pain, you have to be honest about it and accept it. You are not your thoughts, your stories, your trauma, or even your beliefs. You are a complex divine being. As you begin to see yourself more clearly, it enables you to see others more clearly and with compassion. Anything that happens to any being, is happening to you on some level. Your liberation is dependent on the liberation of others, and theirs is dependent on yours.

Self-love is a journey. It is the pathway to freedom. It requires deep healing, truth telling, and self-reflection. What do you need to love yourself more fully? Wounded people cannot express authentic love and be loving. Are you living inside your sorrow and in the depths of your pain? When you wake up in the morning, you are in control of your life choices. Choose love. No one can take it away from you. Choose love. Choose kindness. Choose compassion. Choose to seek the truth. Choose to be you. There will be good days and bad days, but you're writing your own story. You can choose self-love, radical love, and revolutionary love in every moment of every day.

Svadhyaha, self-study, is to examine, reflect, accept and radically love yourself, so you will have the capacity to unconditionally love others. Do the inner work rather than denying or avoiding with spiritual bypassing. Deeply know your Self and awaken to your Truth.

Soul existed before you were born and will exist after you die. You are the soul and the soul is infinite. Shed the fear that hides the light of the soul. ~Unknown

Remembering Your True Self Meditation: I AM

Sit or lie down in a comfortable position
Close your eyes or soften your gaze

Become aware of your breathing
The rise and fall of your chest

Begin to watch your breath
Sense your breath and your body

Inhale, "I"
Exhale, "Am"

Who Am I
You are, at the core, Divine

As you exhale, begin to let go
Peel back outer layers
Release your armor
Let go of your belief system
Let go of how you identify yourself
Let go of your likes and dislikes
And let go of your fears, insecurities, and doubt
Let it all go
With every exhale, let go, more and more

Remember who you are

Remember you are the Divine living inside
Learn to understand the layers wrapped around you
Learn to gradually know yourself more and more
Your true identity
Your True Self
Know yourself so well
That you grow into wholeness
And into your greatness

Inhale, "I"
Exhale, "Am"

Return to gentle, easy breaths through your nose
When you are ready slowly open your eyes

Namaste, and so it is

Svadhyaya ~ Self-Study Reflection Question

1. Reflect on your personal belief system and conditioning with regard to racism, prejudice and bias. Is it still true today? Have you been using yoga or a spiritual practice to avoid your feelings?

2. Have you confused being "nice" or "good" with the idea of not seeing race or color? Have you ever thought or said, "I'm not racist; I don't see color"? Sit with those emotions and then write about them.

3. Is there something holding you back from stepping into your power? What unhealed trauma, beliefs, or fears, if any, are preventing your growth?

4. If you are white, examine your whiteness. How did you learn to be white? What does it mean to be white?

11 Ishvara Pranidhana ~ Surrender

"Although the world is full of suffering, it is also full of the overcoming of it." ~Helen Keller

The fifth Niyama or yoga guideline is Ishvara Pranidhana, a Sanskrit word that means surrender. Ishvara Pranidhana, surrender, is all about living in the moment. There is a rhythmic way of breathing and moving and living. You are not fighting the in-hale or resisting the ex-hale, but you are inviting each breath, just as it is. When you are in alignment, body and breath, you can experience pure joy, bliss and surrender. Cultivate a relationship with the universe and devote your actions to something bigger than yourself. Ishvara Pranidhana means to surrender to your higher self, to cultivate a trusting relationship with the universe, and to connect to something greater than yourself.

The Intersection between Acceptance and Change

There's an art and skill to surrender. Surrender means to stop fighting, stop controlling, and stop getting in the way of what's flowing to you. You still have to put in the work, but from a place of surrender or non-attachment. Go slowly, connect to the pulse of your heart, and follow your intuition. Communication is a dance with the universe; the universe will express the best path for you. Pause if you find yourself trying to control an outcome and consciously shift your energy to surrender. Put in the effort, invest in yourself, and be patient, compassionate and loving.

Clear Mind and Open Heart

Cultivate a heart and mind connection. Slow down. Be present. Be here now. It's impossible to be present and connected when you are too busy. Can you pause and slow down? Can you arrive fully to each moment, just as it is? Connected. Open. Pure. Can you arrive fully and completely present with your children, partner, and colleagues?

Life is fluid; it changes. More effort does not always bring greater results. Smarter strategies bring greater results. Think of an area in your life where you are trying and fighting without making any progress. What would letting go look like? Can you surrender to your anxiety, worry, fear or depression? Can you pause and sit with those feelings and realize they cannot break you? Sit long enough to recognize those feelings are not you. You are not your thoughts or your feelings. Slowly, your emotions will lose a considerable amount of power over you. As you became more aware of your feelings, then you can make a choice about how you respond to life. You are able to live in the present moment and empower yourself to control what you think, say and do. You can begin to respond with love.

The Power of Love

The Power and the Love are in the choices you make. A true yogi will bridge personal transformation and a spiritual practice to social action. They will understand that you cannot just go inside yourself; you must go towards one another. If you are a disingenuous yogi who treats people badly and thinks you are better than everyone else, then you are not being real, or loving, or honest. It doesn't matter how many yoga classes you take, if you can handstand, if you chant, if you are vegan, or if you have traveled to India. What matters is what's in your heart. You cannot hide behind your yoga practice, your religion, or your spirituality.

Bring love and compassion into your attitude and into all your actions. Love is love. Love is an action. Yoga is an action. Anti-racism is an action. Are you moving towards awakening, being love, and making compassionate choices? Are you awakening to the truth? Can you open your heart and see yourself and others with loving eyes?

Letting Go

Letting go is one of the biggest challenges on the spiritual path. Change is difficult because we are not good at letting go. Release the need to control, have faith and trust that the Universe has a plan even greater than you can possibly imagine. The yoga pose savasana, is one of our greatest teachers. It teaches us to let go, both physically and mentally. It teaches us to be content with stillness. It teaches us to listen. You can spend a lifetime fighting yourself and fighting life or you can surrender. You can take off your armor of protection that you don't need any longer and open your heart and mind to the spaciousness of the Universe. Awaken to the moment with wonder, curiosity and a child-like spirit. Stop fighting and begin to make compassionate and loving choices. Have faith and allow the magic to show up.

Let what's meant to happen, happen.

There is a rhythm and flow, an expansion and contraction to life. To surrender is to stop struggling and to learn to live in the moment. When you are so busy with your to-do list, you forget to connect with the rhythm of life, or with God's heartbeat. Practice slowing down, detaching from the outcome, connecting to your heartbeat, watching a sunrise or sunset, enjoying savasana and letting go.

Trust the cyclical nature of life. Rhythm is essential to life. The earth circles the sun, the tide rises and falls, inhale is followed by exhale, life is moment to moment. We will inevitably go through phases like the moon: re-birth and death, rise and release, expansion and contraction, cycles and rhythms. Honor the cycles of your body, energy levels, and emotions. You have a rhythm and prana, or life force, central to your well-being. Avoid over scheduling yourself, causing anxiety and stress. Instead, attune to your prana and create a harmonious space around you. Cultivate a spiritually fulfilling life by making better choices about how you think, shape your days, nourish your body and nurture relationships.

If It's Not a Yes, Then It's a No. Practice Saying, No.

Don't let the fear of being judged or disliked stop you from being yourself or from doing what's right for yourself and others. Have the courage to be disliked. Surrender to the truth and if the truth is a no, say no. As Deborah Adele[25] writes, "Surrender is not passive." It takes strength and courage to stand up and do what's right for yourself and others. Surrender means understanding the needs of the moment and dedicating yourself to a higher purpose.

Search for Meaning in Your Life

"And the day came when the risk to remain tight in a bud was more painful than the risk it took to blossom." ~Anais Nin

Everyone can live for a greater cause. We are all great in our own way. It doesn't really matter what it is, as long as you're living for a purpose bigger than yourself. Life is better when you have a purpose that goes beyond your own material needs. It may be religious, political, for civil rights or any social issue or cause. It is a reason to be passionate about life, a reason to get up in the morning. Find a way to contribute to the world, and you will receive immense satisfaction. Aim to truly make the world, or simply your neighborhood, a better place, and live for a cause that makes your life, and the lives of others, better. You do not need to be Harriet Tubman. It does not need to be a big heroic act; it can be a small, simple, impactful act. You do not have to

---

[25] Deborah Adele is the author of the book *The Yamas & Niyamas: Exploring Yoga's Ethical Practice.*

be anything or do anything other than to awaken to who you are right now. You are an infinite being of light. Remember, your light is living inside. Your passion may be the spark that ignites someone else to step into their power. Choose a path you would like to travel in order to seek meaning, purpose, and significance.

Struggle Reveals Your True Self

Struggle is inevitable at some point in all our lives. Struggle is necessary for you to grow and expand into your Highest Self. Throughout life, you will struggle and suffer whenever you do not get what you want or when you're not in control. If you do not surrender and transform suffering, you will carry the burden with you; it will continue to cause distress and you will pass it on to another. If you are invested in alleviating the suffering in the world, you must first awaken to your own suffering. Through every struggle, you become stronger and you can use that experience to realize your true potential and actualize your full humanity.

Black American women have experienced a particularly painful marginalization: we suffer from the double burden of being Black and female in a nation that has always given priority to the experience of white and male. Black women are both Black and female, and thus subject to discrimination on the basis of both race, gender, and often a combination of the two. America has largely ignored the history of oppression of Black women. Intersectionality[26] is a lens through which you are able to see what happens to individuals who are subject to

---

[26] Kimberlé Williams Crenshaw is an American lawyer, civil rights advocate and a leading scholar of critical race theory who developed the theory of intersectionality.

overlapping systems of discrimination.The trauma of intersectionality is killing Black women. Racial violence is killing Black women and men. Say their names: Sandra Bland, Philando Castile, Eric Garner, Freddie Gray, Walter L. Scott, Alton B Sterling, Tamir Rice, John Crawford III, Oscar Grant, Stephon Clark, Michael Brown, Botham Jean, and more. They were all unjustly killed by the police due to the color of their skin.

If you see injustices in the world or witness oppression, it's important not to turn a blind eye. Whether you are the oppressor or the oppressed, we are all impacted in some way.

How do we create real sustainable change for oppressed people?

You start with a willingness to see the truth and with a desire to transform yourself and systems at the institutional level. It will take active work to dismantle systems of oppression. Think critically about racism in the spaces you inhabit. Adopt an intersectional approach in all aspects of your life. All forms of oppression are connected. You cannot fight against one form of injustice and not fight against others.

Anti-racism practice is moment to moment. In any given moment, you will need to pause, reflect and ask yourself, "Am I being racist?" It is not a fixed arrival; it is a continuous practice and a lifelong journey.

Returning to Ritual

Black people have forever used their artistry to transform suffering into beauty. We can look at the many works of Black writers, singers, dancers, painters, inventors, and more. Ruth King[27] writes about using artistry as cultural medicine. This goes beyond self-care, using artistry as a mindfulness practice to express and heal ourselves and the world. Art is like therapy, healing our broken hearts. Inside of you is something you need to express; for Black people it is a way of being heard and seen in a world that has forgotten and ignored us and our gifts. When you transform suffering into a gift for the collective good, you inspire hope and harmony. It is a simple act of consciously and joyfully returning to ritual. Rituals are tools that give us freedom, direction and purpose. Cultivate new rituals or daily habits that help you to transform from the inside out.

Purposeful Living

What do you benefit if you gain the whole world but lose your own soul? Is anything worth more than your soul?
(Matthew 16:26)

Strive for something that is bigger than you. Surrender to a higher purpose. Your higher purpose is how you find deep meaning and fulfillment in your life and how you realize your true potential. Lasting happiness cannot be bought or attained by instant gratification, power, or possessions. Lasting happiness and peace of mind are achieved by devotion to a higher purpose.

---

[27] Ruth King is an insight meditation teacher, life coach, and author of *Healing Rage: Women Making Inner Peace Possible* and *Mindful of Race: Transforming Racism from the Inside Out.*

B.K.S. Iyengar[28] said, "my body is my temple and the asanas (poses) are my prayers." Prayer illuminates your faith and spirituality. It allows you to be in communication with God or a Higher Power. Reflecting on God, your faith, this moment, will help you harmonize and align with Divine will. You will not lose yourself; you will awaken to your truth.

Wake up. Smile. Take a deep cleansing breath. Allow your heart to expand. Pause and listen. Breathe gently. Allow yourself to connect to the Universe, Higher Power, or God. Allow love into your heart. Allow God into your life.

Ishvara Pranidhana encourages you to surrender and live in the moment, to understand rhythm and ritual, to cultivate a deep and trusting relationship with the universe, and to devote yourself to a Higher Purpose.

---

[28] B.K.S. Iyengar, is the founder of the style of modern yoga known as Iyengar yoga and is considered one of the foremost yoga teachers in the world.

The Power of Surrender Meditation: The Rhythm of Surrender

Sit or lie down in a comfortable position
Close your eyes or soften you gaze

Become aware of your breathing
The rise and fall of your chest

Connect to your breath
Connect to your heart center

Feel the pulse of your heart
Breathe into your heart
Let love in
Let God in

Let go
And surrender
To the rhythm
To the flow of life

Imagine a sunrise or sunset
Climbing a mountain
Enjoying the ocean
Practicing yoga and ending with a deep and restful savasana

Arrive fully in this moment

This is the rhythm of surrender

Expand and contract your abdomen
Create spaciousness at the heart center
And throughout your entire body

Pay close attention to the moment
Pay attention to your inner world
Pay attention to the world around you
Ride the wave of the breath
Move with what the moment gives you

What is life asking of you?

Flow with the current of life
This is the rhythm of surrender

Breathe gentle easy breaths through your nose
Deeply relaxed and fully awake
In the moment

When you are ready, slowly open your eyes

Namaste, and so it is

Ishvara Pranidhana ~ Surrender Reflection Questions

1. In what areas, if any, are you fighting with life? Is there someone or something in your life you are trying to control? If so, why? What are you afraid will happen if you let go of your control and surrender?

2. Are you living true to yourself? What practices can you use to deepen the connection to your inner being?

3. Are you doing whatever you can, however big or small, to change the world? If not, what is stopping you? What are you waiting for?

4. Explore three things you can do to begin an anti-racism practice?

Believe in something greater than you and let that guide you.

12 Niyama Review

The Niyamas

The Niyamas, or observances, are guidelines that teach you how to live in peace and harmony with yourself. Following these guidelines allows you to become more mindful of recognizing racism within yourself and in the world. Practicing the Niyamas guides you toward letting go of limiting, harmful and racist behaviors and beliefs.

Niyama Review

SAUCHA: PURITY

Reminder of pure and compassionate thoughts, speech and actions. It is about removing toxins from your heart, body, mind, soul and surroundings, to reveal your shine, your True Self. Saucha journey is about embracing who you are, your core essence.

SANTOSHA: CONTENTMENT

Reminds you to focus on abundance and gratitude to become less self-centered and less white-centered. Cultivate a deep sense of gratitude, and love others, yourself and your life, just as it is.

TAPAS: SELF-DISCIPLINE

Consciously choosing to go through the fire in order to grow and reach your full potential. It reminds you to transform your lessons into blessings, and of the importance of courage, discipline, practice, and facing your fears.

SVADHYAYA: SELF-STUDY

Examine, reflect, accept and radically love yourself, so you will have the capacity to unconditionally love others. Do the inner work rather than denying or avoiding with spiritual bypassing. Deeply know your Self and awaken to your Truth.

ISHVARA PRANIDHANA: SURRENDER

Encourages you to surrender and live in the moment, to understand rhythm and ritual, to cultivate a deep and trusting relationship with the universe, and to devote yourself to a Higher Purpose.

13 Your Life's Journey

"...Be a bush if you can't be a tree. If you can't be a highway, just be a trail. If you can't be a sun, be a star. For it isn't by size that you win or fail. Be the best of whatever you are."
~Dr. Martin Luther King Jr.

Your Life's AntiRacism Blueprint

These guidelines, the Yamas and Niyamas, serve as your life's anti-racism blueprint. Following the guidelines will help you to cultivate an anti-racism practice. They help you to trust the process of discovering your true authentic Self and to align with your life's purpose. You must nurture your soul, your personal and spiritual growth daily.

The Yamas teach you how to truly live in harmony with the world. The Niyamas increase mindfulness, and open you up to all the possibilities and full potential of your life. You are in the process of clearly seeing systemic and institutionalized racism. Now you have a solid blueprint to build a strong foundation for inner and outer change. As you practice, you will continue to build a deep belief in yourself and in your ability to create positive change. What is your life's legacy? What is your dharma? What is your vision for justice and equality? Follow your truth with an open mind and an open heart.

Following your life's anti-racism blueprint does not mean that things will always go your way. It means you will have the tools to overcome whatever you encounter on your path. Welcome your mistakes and failures as an opportunity to grow and learn. Celebrate your successes, no matter how big or small.

Turn Love into a Political and Social Force

Awakening to anti-racism and integrating anti-racism into your yoga practice is an essential component for achieving liberation. To create positive change and forward movement, denial isn't the answer. We live in a profoundly separate and unequal world. White supremacy is built into the foundation of America, as well as the world. It's not enough to be non-racist; white supremacy will continue even without individual racists. To overcome oppression and create a more just world, there needs to be mass participation in transforming basic systems in ways that will distribute power differently. There is important individual healing work to be done, before many are able to contribute to an anti-racist movement. The practice of yoga and anti-racism has the potential to provide healing to ourselves and to the world.

Yoga for Social Change

"We must always take sides. Neutrality helps the oppressor, never the victim. Silence encourages the tormentor, never the tormented." ~Elie Wiesel

There's a lot of heavy, painful and heartbreaking things happening in the United States and throughout the world. So much of the world reflects sexism, homophobia and racism. Colonization left a legacy of oppression that continues throughout the world today. Racist and sexist ideas and actions result from oppression. This is how our country began — oppression, abuse, violence, terrorism.

America was built on racism. We are not trying to "make America great again." The America we want, the promise of liberty and justice for all, is the America yet to be achieved. We are in the process of reimagining America. We are trying to make the entire world a more just place.

What is your vision for a just world? What world do you wish to create? My vision is to live in a world that truly sees all people, celebrates our differences and works to create fairness and justice for all. If that too is yours, let's work to create a world where people of all races, religions, socioeconomic classes, sexual orientations, gender identities and abilities are seen as human beings and treated equally. Yogic principles can be practiced to create social change throughout the world. We can steadily change the world we live in through self-reflection, deep healing, and right or compassionate action.

Ally Is a Verb

Fifty years after the end of the civil rights movement, it remains a radical and revolutionary act to be a white ally. The more of us who stand up to end racism and all forms of oppression, the more power we have to change the world —one person, one life, one small compassionate act at a time.

Use your privilege and power compassionately: become an effective ally. Support, learn from, listen to understand, and act collaboratively with those who are typically silenced, disempowered and oppressed. It's important to cultivate an anti-racism practice that is not self-serving. White saviorism[29] is narcissistic and extremely problematic.

Avoid performative allyship and activism. Performative activism is when you make your actions and contributions about you instead of about the marginalized group of people. Performative allyship could be a lot of talk, rants and social media likes, comments and posts with not nearly enough action. Action is necessary to create change. Action begins with calling yourself out.

Reverend angel Kyodo Williams explains that, "True allyship is not possible without relationship." Yoga means union and ally means to unite and form a connection. Build a relationship where your privilege intersects with someone else's oppression. Being an ally is more than being sympathetic towards those who experience discrimination. Oppressed people don't need another apology without action. Being an ally is more than simply believing in equality. It means being willing to

---

[29] White saviorism refers to a white person who acts to help non-white people in a self-serving way, without doing any research, asking any questions, or reflecting carefully.

act with and for others with the goal of ending oppression and creating equality. Compassion is not enough, you must take action.

Allyship is a continuous practice. Your work and call to action should center the voices and needs of those most critically impacted. An awakening is needed, then change, and collaborative rebuilding. Closely examine how you can contribute to creating change using your platform, privilege and power. Are you hiring or working collaboratively with other BIPOC? Are you advocating for BIPOC to be hired? Are you opening up spaces without taking them over? As a white ally, are you spreading awareness and holding people accountable in your own circle or community?

Here are some steps you can take to begin living as a white ally (adapted from Unitarian Universalist Association):

- Learn the truth about the racist history of our country.
- Take responsibility for your own racial identity journey.
- Work to change racist institutions.
- Be an accountable ally to BIPOC.
- Nurture a positive anti-racist white identity in children.
- Build a white anti-racist collective.

We are all part of a system built to oppress. It lives because of ignorance, apathy and unawareness. We all have a role to play in making it better. Take action, do the work of dismantling racism and transform racism from the inside out.

"We are not fully evolved as human beings until we care about universal human rights. ...We all have a responsibility to create a just society." ~Bryan Stevenson

Epilogue

"We did not come to fear the future. We came here to shape it."
~Barack Obama

Faith, Courage and Wisdom

F aith is an internal feeling, a sense that there is something more. A sense that things will get better. I've recognized that writing is an act of faith for me. I started writing consistently around the age of 12. It was an act of hope for me, a hope that things could get better. It was a place to put my pain, grief and despair, so I didn't have to carry it with me everywhere. Writing, and eventually sharing my stories, was an act of faith. I wasn't broken. I was slowly getting stronger. My story or your story may be the key to unlocking someone else's pain or helping someone find their sense of authenticity and freedom. Your truth, your compassion, and your right action have the power to awaken others.

Choose a path you would like to travel in order to seek meaning and purpose in your life. Put in the effort, activate your spirituality, and invest in yourself. Have faith, and in the words of Jesse Jackson, "Keep hope alive."

How do you connect to your inner source, your inner being?

Our intention is to connect to our inner being, our soul. Inside of us is the being that God has already created: the Christ, the Messiah, the Buddha, the Enlightened One, the Atman, our Essence.

There are many paths and ways to travel inward to experience your soul. This is a lifelong journey.

• Aspire to grow daily. Don't go through day-to-day moments. Be present and *grow* through day-to-day moments. Look for the lessons.

• Heighten your self-awareness. Seek to discover who you truly are, express what you are experiencing from the heart, write down your intentions, self-reflect daily, meditate, practice compassion and mindfulness and be open to listening to others.

• Provide time for healing and discernment. Let go of willful ignorance by asking questions and seeking answers. Choose to not be blind. Choose to accept the often painful truth. Choose to talk about difficult things like gun control, oppression and inequality. Talk with the people you disagree with and seek to understand their point of view, while also seeing them as worthy of love and respect.

• Unity of thought, word and action. Bliss lies within unity. Your word is bond. Be real, honest, and truthful in thought, word and action. There is no doubt in what is being said, heard or seen. Your thoughts, words and actions are in alignment.

Universal Truth

The socially conscious mind practices global mindfulness. When you become conscious and truthful about what's going on around you, you will experience a greater sense of self. You will make an effort to be a more compassionate person and to take better care of yourself and the global community. Compassion causes you to feel deeply for people and stirs a desire to ease the suffering in the world. The suffering of one is the suffering of all. Now is the time to take compassionate action.

Inspired To Learn More

Books:

Yoga Sutras of Patanjali by Sri Swami Satchidananda

The Bhagavad Gita: A New Translation by Stephen Mitchell

The Yamas & Niyamas: Exploring Yoga's Ethical Practice by Deborah Adele

The New Jim Crow: Mass Incarceration in the Age of Colorblindness by Michelle Alexander

Between the World and Me by Ta-Nehisi Coates

Radical Dharma: Talking Race, Love. and Liberation by Rev. angel Kyodo Williams, Lama Rod Owens and Jasmine Syedullah Ph.D

Writing as a Way of Healing: How Telling Our Stories Transforms Our Lives by Louise Desalvo

The Souls of Black Folk by Dr. W. E. B. Du Bois

White Fragility: Why It's So Hard for White People to Talk about Racism by Robin DiAngelo

The Warmth of Other Suns: The Epic Story of America's Great Migration by Isabel Wilkerson

The Four Agreements: A Practical Guide to Personal Freedom by Don Miguel Ruiz

A Return to Love: Reflections on the Principles of "A Course in Miracles" by Marianne Williamson

Homegoing by Yaa Gyasi

Mindful of Race: Transforming Racism from the Inside Out by Ruth King

Skill in Action: Radicalizing Your Yoga Practice to Create a Just World by Michelle Cassandra Johnson

Me and White Supremacy by Layla Saad

Just Mercy: A Story of Justice and Redemption by Bryan Stevenson

Stamped from the Beginning: The Definitive History of Racist Ideas In America by Ibram X. Kendi

So You Want to Talk About Race by Ijeoma Oluo

Films:

Sorry to Bother You Directed by Boots Riley

13th Amendment Directed by Ava DuVernay

Fruitvale Station Directed by Ryan Coogler

When They See Us Created and Directed by Ava DuVernay

Podcasts:

Scene on Radio Podcast: "Seeing White" Series

On Being Podcast with Krista Tippet: Claudia Rankine — "How Can I Say This So We Can Stay in This Car Together?" and "Eula Biss — Let's Talk About Whiteness."

CTZN Podcast: "Rachel Cargle," "Dr. Robin DiAngelo" and "Rev angel Kyodo Williams"

Commune: "You're (Still) A Little Bit Racist"

10% Happier with Dan Harris: "Ruth King, Being Mindful of Race"

Awaken to your life and everything becomes an opportunity to learn and grow.

Acknowledgements

W riting this book has been a journey of both pain and healing. I continue to put the pieces of myself together through yoga, writing and self-reflections. Deep gratitude for my African ancestors who were kidnapped, shackled, taken onto a slave ship, and brought to America as free labor. Their strength and willpower reside in me. Thank you to my Mexican and Spanish ancestors who endured difficult times yet made it possible for my grandparents to come to America for a better life. Thank you to Deborah Adele, her book *The Yamas & Niyamas*, deeply inspired me. Namaste to each and every yoga teacher who faithfully taught me the beauty of what their teachers shared with them. Gratitude for my faithful yoga students who show up on their mats with open hearts and minds. Grateful heart for Gray and Blythe Buetzow and Yael Weiss for your devotion, love and support. Much love and gratitude to my parents, Joanne Marquez and Leon Swindell, who endured the trials and tribulations of an interracial marriage for eighteen years and helped shaped me into the awakened love warrior woman I am today. Thank you to my mom who loves unconditionally and shows me by example how transformation happens from the inside out. Gratitude to Neil Stadtmore who was brave enough to read the very first draft and provided me with honest yet loving feedback. Much gratitude to an amazing ally, Kim Bradle of Jaya Yoga. Her belief in me and in this work kept me going, even when I thought no one cared and I wanted to give up. Thank you to all the women of Lady Magic who hold space for me to laugh uncontrollably and to be loved unconditionally. Gratitude to Kysha Mitchell who coached me up with confidence in the very early stages of this book. Deep gratitude to my bestie Kendra Barnes who always shows up for me. As my sister said, "Everyone needs a Kendra in their life." Love and deep gratitude to my friend and magic sister, Delina Brooks, who never ceases to amaze me with her wisdom, artistry, and generous heart. Thank you so much for all the care and time you put into helping make this book have a heartbeat.

My fiercest love and gratitude to my husband and children, Demetrius, Xavier and Simone. To my husband for his unwavering belief in me. To Xavier and Simone for your love and support and for challenging me to always be my best.

About The Author

S onia Roberts is an educator, writer and certified yoga teacher with twenty years of teaching experience. She has a strong desire to create social change and to support people in reaching their full potential. Her yoga classes are challenging and nurturing, and they integrate mindful movement. She has always been drawn to movement, first with dance and then with yoga, as a way to align and deeply connect to breath and body.

Sonia is a graduate of the Piedmont Yoga 750-hour Advanced Studies Program, studying with Richard Rosen, Rodney Yee, Clare Finn and Maritza. She has completed YogaWorks 200-hour teacher training with Mynx Inatsugu and Melanie Salvatore-August. Sonia also completed Jane Austin's Pre-Natal Yoga Teacher Training at Yoga Tree in San Francisco. As a lifelong student of yoga, she has completed a variety of workshops with master yoga teachers and enjoys continuing her yoga education. Her training has been influenced by many teachers and traditions, including Iyengar, Ashtanga, Vinyasa and Anusara.

Sonia has a Bachelor of Arts degree in Social Welfare and Dance Minor from UC Berkeley. She has worked for several non-profit organizations in both the Bay Area and Los Angeles, as a counselor and educator. Her passions for yoga and social justice connect to create deep healing and transformation both personally and globally.

Her life as a wife and mother has given her an abundance of opportunity for deepening her yoga practice and living in the moment. Sonia is devoted to supporting others to awaken to their true self and to steadily change the world we live in through yoga, meditation, writing, and self-reflection.

Visit www.awkenedlovewarrior.com to learn more and to sign up for our email list.

Love Note

I wish you a life journey full of love, courage, healing light, deep heart connections, surrender and enough compassion to create positive change in your life and in the world. May the journey to discovering the truth of who you are bring you lasting joy and inspire others to do the same.

Lokah Samastah Sukhino Bhavantu

May all beings be happy and free, and may the thoughts, words and actions of my own life contribute in some way to that happiness and freedom for all.

Ase, Namaste, Amen and so it is.

Made in the USA
Monee, IL
17 June 2020

34102615R00094